RUTGERS PROFESSIONAL PSYCHOLOGY REVIEW

Volume 1:
Educating Professional Psychologists

Volume 1:
Educating Professional Psychologists

GUEST EDITORS: Glenn R. Caddy
David C. Rimm
Neill Watson
James H. Johnson

RUTGERS PROFESSIONAL PSYCHOLOGY REVIEW

The Graduate School of Applied and Professional Psychology,
Rutgers—The State University of New Jersey

Transaction Books
New Brunswick (U.S.A.) and London (U.K.)

ISBN: 0-87855-449-1
ISSN: 0277-4240
Printed in the United States of America

On the Form and Future of the
Rutgers Professional Psychology Review

With this volume, the *Rutgers Professional Psychology Review* is inaugurated as an annual of conference and symposium reports in professional psychology. The current issue reports the Virginia Beach conference on the education of professional psychologists. This was the first nationally representative conference in which leaders of programs expressly designed to train practitioners of psychology met to consider the problems of student admission, faculty composition, curriculum content, practicum training, administrative organization, and accreditation that challenge anyone who sets out to educate psychologists for careers of professional service. The conference was organized by David C. Rimm and colleagues then at Old Dominion University in Norfolk, Virginia. A statement on the emergence of professional psychology was written later by Glenn R. Caddy, and the entire conference report was edited by Glenn Caddy, David Rimm, Neill Watson, and James Johnson, all affiliated at the time with the newly-founded Virginia consortium in professional psychology.

The general plan for future issues is well defined. We will report conferences and symposia at the forefront of professional psychology. Two members of our editorial board are centrally involved in organizing conferences of the kind that would furnish ideal material for the *Review*. In developing symposia, we will adapt the procedures and format of such annuals as the *Nebraska Symposia on Motivation* to the aims and substance of professional psychology. Announcement of specific contents would be premature at this time, but the potential supply of excellent material seems abundant. In future issues, we intend to present material that is at least dependable and useful, and at most creative and inspiring.

The *Review* began as a student project. Edward Adams, Psy.D. 1979, took the main initiative in founding the journal as a "forum for the dissemination of information relevant to the needs and concerns of students and faculty of the Graduate School of Applied and Professional Psychology." Andrea Bishop edited the first issue for 1979. This predecessor of the present *Review* was of local interest by design and is no longer available. The second issue, for 1980, was composed of invited articles of general interest on licensure and credentialling in professional psychology. Editorial work was done by Margaret M. Eaton and Frances P. Snepp. Funds were provided by the Rutgers University Graduate Student Organization and the Advisory Associates of the Graduate School of Applied and Professional Psychology. Contents of the 1980 issue are shown on page 180 of the current volume. As of this writing, copies can still be obtained.

With the present volume, we move to a new form in the evolution of the *Review*. We believe the material we present will interest professional psychologists. Since we view professional psychology as the application of disciplined knowledge about psychological processes to the understanding and solution of human problems, some of the material we offer should also be of interest to psychologists in general. Since professional psychology is only one of the disciplines concerned with human problems, psychiatrists, social workers, special educators, and those in other human service professions may also find value in some of the contents. Since we are all engaged in efforts to comprehend and alleviate human distress, some of our presentations may be of general public concern. We shall see about that. For the moment, we are proud to present the first conference ever conducted on the direct education of professional psychologists.

Donald R. Peterson
Editor

RUTGERS PROFESSIONAL PSYCHOLOGY REVIEW
Volume 1, 1982

EDUCATING PROFESSIONAL PSYCHOLOGISTS

Edited by

Glenn R. Caddy, David C. Rimm, Neill Watson,
and James H. Johnson

Virginia Consortium for Professional Psychology
Norfolk and Williamsburg, Virginia

The Proceedings of the Virginia Beach Conference on Education
in Professional Psychology: And Beyond

Contributors

Glenn R. Caddy, Ph.D., associate professor, Department of Psychology, Old Dominion University, and Department of Psychiatry and Behavioral Sciences, Eastern Virginia Medical School, Norfolk, Virginia.

Meredith Crawford, Ph.D., accreditation officer, American Psychological Association, Washington, D.C.

Clifford M. DeCato, Ph.D., associate director of graduate education in psychology, Hahnemann Medical College and Hospital, Philadelphia, Pennsylvania.

Daniel B. Fishman, Ph.D., associate professor and director of psychological services, Graduate School of Applied and Professional Psychology, Rutgers University, New Brunswick, New Jersey.

Ronald E. Fox, Ph.D., dean, School of Professional Psychology, Wright State University, Dayton, Ohio.

Ronald Giannetti, Ph.D., director of Psychology Internship Program, Department of Psychiatry and Behavioral Sciences, Eastern Virginia Medical School, Norfolk, Virginia.

James H. Johnson, Ph.D., professor and director of clinical training, Illinois Institute of Technology, Chicago, Illinois.

Joy Kanarkat, Ph.D., associate professor of psychology, Department of Psychology, Norfolk State University, Norfolk, Virginia.

Arthur Kovacs, Ph.D., professor of psychology, The California School of Professional Psychology, Los Angeles, California.

Donald R. Peterson, Ph.D., dean, Graduate School of Applied and Professional Psychology, Rutgers University, New Brunswick, New Jersey.

David C. Rimm, Ph.D., professor, Department of Psychology, North Texas State University, Denton, Texas.

David A. Rodgers, Ph.D., chief psychologist, Cleveland Clinic, Cleveland, Ohio.

Rashad Saafir, Ph.D., professor, Department of Psychology, Norfolk State University, Norfolk, Virginia.

Donald T. Shannon, Ph.D., associate professor of psychology, University of Illinois, Champaign-Urbana, Illinois.

Mac Sterling, Ph.D., professor of psychology, Baylor University, Waco, Texas.

Neill Watson, Ph.D., assistant professor, Department of Psychology, The College of William and Mary, Williamsburg, Virginia.

Wallace W. Wilkins, Ph.D., professor and director of clinical training, Department of Psychology, Old Dominion University, Norfolk, Virginia.

Table of Contents

But in the final analysis the progress of clinical psychology, as of every other science, will be determined by the value and amount of its contributions to the advancement of the human race.

Lightner Witmer, 1907

Preface

A conference on education in professional psychology was held at Virginia Beach, Virginia, April 27–29, 1978. This conference was convened and chaired by Dr. David C. Rimm and sponsored by the newly-formed Virginia Consortium for Professional Psychology, which initiated a Doctor of Psychology program in clinical psychology in the fall of 1978. Anticipating the introduction of yet one more new program in this rapidly expanding field, the Virginia consortium believed that the field generally could derive considerable value from exploring the recent developments in practitioner-model programs in professional psychology,[1,2] as well as examining the question of standards in program quality and control. This book provides an account of that conference, the issues and questions raised during the actual proceedings, and the resolutions debated and passed during those three hectic days. It also provides some continuing perspective by examining briefly a number of the more significant developments that have occurred within professional psychology during the two years immediately following the conference.

Unlike any of the previous conferences addressing the education of psychologists (see for example, Hoch, Ross, & Winder, 1966; Korman, 1976; and Raimy, 1950), the Virginia Beach conference involved participants who, by and large, were committed to the practitioner model of education. Yet, the conference was anything but a forum designed to provide unconditional support for the further development of that particular educational approach. Certainly, many of the conferees were enthusiastic about the developments within psychology that they were witnessing and in which they were participating. This enthusiasm was balanced by what generally was seen to be the serious need to examine the nature and the impact of the recent developments within professional psychology. There was a desire to learn from one another, there was a search for common ground and direction, and there was a desire to explore the prospects of achieving some consensus about the professionalizing of psychology. There was a need for data and there was a need for speculation.

During the planning of the conference the decision was made to focus the proceedings on an examination of the developments and technologies available within the currently existing practitioner-model educational programs, for it was believed that such an examination would be most valuable and timely. The planning committee [3] sought to explore issues of admission, curriculum, practicum training, and other aspects of the educational process including accreditation. Further, we saw the need to explore a number of other important issues that we considered worthy of consideration by our profession at this time. For example, we were concerned about the extent of the need within our society for professional psychologists, and we wondered about how many graduates would be produced by the proliferation of programs providing such training. We wondered also about the effects on our society and our profession that such increased numbers of psychologists entering the service delivery arena would produce. We reflected concern over quality control and, in particular, on the criteria that would be established for those institutions seeking to provide professionally-oriented educational programs in psychology. Furthermore, we sought to examine the views of the conferees regarding the type of institution they considered likely to provide the best prospects for ensuring excellence in the professionally-oriented educational process.

There were other questions that we felt were important to be raised, but which we felt should be the focus of another conference in another context. For example, given what we were perceiving as the explosive expansion of practitioner-model programs, we wondered how the public and other professions would view psychology if it permitted rapid growth without providing some rather definitive controls in the form of professional standards directed at the institutions which were producing this new army of professional psychologists. Related to this issue, we wondered whether the rapid expansion of professional psychology training programs would bring with it the erosion of excellence about which some have reflected such grave concerns when focusing upon the more traditional training approach. Most importantly, we pondered over just who would benefit most from the developments within professional psychology. We asked, for example, if the professional psychologists trained in such programs would begin to serve those in our society who traditionally have been disenfranchised from the mental health delivery system or whether, like many in the medical and other professions, they would choose to focus their energies in employment that would bring the maximum financial return for their educational investment.

Finally, we considered that this conference, like the other training conferences that preceded it, would do well to offer those within our discipline a set of resolutions designed to reflect some general consensus and to recommend within these resolutions a set of guidelines for those conducting practitioner-model educational programs in professional psychology in the future.

In selecting the people who would be invited to participate in the conference, the planning committee looked for individuals who could represent well the state of the art in the various types of practitioner-model programs that currently existed or were being planned, as well as others who were known to have a particularly strong interest in this model of clinical training. The idea was to invite a relatively small group of people to a working conference from which, hopefully, would come a number of positions relevant to the entire field.

The principal speakers at the Virginia Beach conference were: Dr. Clifford M. DeCato, associate director, Graduate Education in Psychology, Hahnemann Medical College; Dr. Gordon Derner, dean, Institute of Advanced Psychological Studies, Adelphi University; Dr. Daniel B. Fishman, director of psychological services, Graduate School of Applied and Professional Psychology, Rutgers University; Dr. Ronald E. Fox, dean, School of Professional Psychology, Wright State University; Dr. Carolyn Jackson, administrative officer for accreditation, Office of Educational Affairs, American Psychological Association; Dr. Arthur Kovacs, dean, California School of Professional Psychology; Dr. Donald R. Peterson, dean, Graduate School of Applied and Professional Psychology, Rutgers University; Dr. David C. Rimm, director of clinical training in psychology, Old Dominion University; Dr. Donald T. Shannon, director of clinical training in psychology, University of Illinois (Champaign-Urbana); and Dr. Mac Sterling, director, Doctor of Psychology Program, Baylor University.

The invited participants to the conference were: Dr. Richard Abidin, director, School/Child-Clinical Program, University of Virginia; Dr. Kent Bailey, director of clinical training, Virginia Commonwealth University; Dr. Glenn R. Caddy, codirector, Virginia Consortium for Professional Psychology; Dr. Jacob Chwast, chairman, Professional School Committee, New York Society of Clinical Psychology; Dr. Richard M. Eisler, director of clinical training in psychology, Virginia Polytechnical Institute; Dr. Charles Flowers, executive assistant to the president, Norfolk State University; Dr. Raymond D. Fowler, chairman of psychology, University of Alabama; Dr. David Hager, dean, School of Graduate Studies, Old Dominion University; Dr. E. Rae Harcum, chairman of psychology, The College of William and Mary; Dr. Bill Hawkins, chairman of psychology, Central Michigan University; Dr. James H. Johnson, codirector, Virginia Consortium for Professional Psychology; Dr. Hugh McLeod, chairman of psychology, Lakehead University; Dr. Carl E. Morgan, president, Illinois School of Professional Psychology; Dr. N. Dickon Reppucci, director of graduate training in community and clinical psychology, University of Virginia; Dr. William Scarpetti, director of psychology, Department of Psychiatry and Behavioral Sciences, Eastern Virginia Medical School; Dr. Glenn Shean, professor of psychology, The College of William and Mary; Dr. Pierre Ventur, member of the Coordinating Committee, Long Island School of Professional Psychology; Dr. Neill Watson, codirector, Virginia Consortium for Professional Psychology; Dr. Bruce J. Weiss, program director, Massachusetts School of Professional Psychology; and Dr. Harl Young, professor, School of Professional Psychology, University of Denver.

This book does not offer a particularly detailed account of the proceedings of the Virginia Beach conference nor is it our intention to provide an extremely comprehensive review of all of the currently functioning programs in professional psychology. Rather, the emphasis of the conference and of this book on the practitioner model of education in clinical psychology reflects the fact that the practitioner model has been developed primarily within clinical psychology. Nevertheless, we believe that the issues examined are very important to all of the specialties in professional psychology. We have sought to focus in some detail on a limited number of what we consider to be representative programs and what we regard as major issues in professional psychology, many of which were discussed at the conference. Further, in order to provide as up-to-date a perspective as possible on the continuing developments within professional psychology and the evaluation of the issues examined at the conference, we have included material not available at the time of the conference and perspectives that only time can provide. The book is divided into four parts. Part A examines the emergence of professional psychology and reviews both background information and recent developments thus setting the context of the conference. Part B overviews the development and growth of the Doctor of Psychology degree and offers guidance on topics including entrance requirements, student selection procedures, practicum development, and curriculum design in professional programming. Part C offers examples of professional program models operating in various administrative settings and presents some of the issues that these various settings create for the programs they support. Finally, Part D contains the resolutions of the Virginia Beach conference and reflects on the implications of these resolutions and provides some speculation on likely developments within professional psychology in the immediate future.

In closing this preface we would like to take this opportunity to thank all of the conference participants for making those three hectic days so stimulating and so provocative. In addition, we would like to express our appreciation to Dr. Charles Burgess, academic vice president and provost of Old Dominion University; Dr. Gerald Holman, dean, Eastern Virginia Medical School; and Dr. George Healy, vice president for academic affairs, The College of William and Mary, who provided the financial support necessary to conduct the conference. Last, we would be remiss if we did not acknowledge the tireless and continuous effort expended by Mrs. Beverly Stanley, who has been a part of every phase of the development of this project. Mrs. Stanley did everything from the coordinating of travel arrangements for the conference to the typing of this manuscript. Her assistance has been invaluable.

> Glenn R. Caddy
> David C. Rimm
> Neill Watson
> James H. Johnson

Norfolk, Virginia
June, 1980

Notes

1. The term "professional" is used to refer to the delivery of psychological services. The term "practitioner model," as distinguished from the "scientist-practitioner model," is used to refer to the alternative type of education in professional psychology advocated at the Vail conference.
2. The field of "professional psychology" encompasses the specialties of clinical, counseling, school, and industrial/organizational psychology. The Virginia Beach conference and this book will focus on the clinical specialty within professional psychology.
3. This committee consisted of Glenn R. Caddy, James H. Johnson, David C. Rimm, and Neill Watson.

References

Hoch, E. L., Ross, A. O., & Winder, C. L. (Eds.) *Professional preparation of clinical psychologists: Proceedings of the conference on the professional preparation of clinical psychologists meeting at the Center for Continuing Education. Chicago, Illinois, August 27–September 1, 1965.* Washington, D. C.: American Psychological Association, 1966.

Korman, M. (Ed.) *Levels and patterns of professional training in psychology: Conference proceedings, Vail, Colorado, July 25-30, 1973.* Washington, D. C.: American Psychological Association, 1976.

Raimy, V. (Ed.) *Training in clinical psychology* (by the staff of the Conference on Graduate Education in Clinical Psychology held at Boulder, Colorado, in August of 1949). New York: Prentice-Hall, 1950.

PART A
Introduction

CHAPTER 1

The Emergence of Professional Psychology: Background to the Virginia Beach Conference and Beyond

Glenn R. Caddy
Virginia Consortium for Professional Psychology

In this portrayal of the emergence of professional psychology, Dr. Caddy raises briefly the major issues and concerns that faced the participants at the Virginia Beach conference and continue to require examination and action at the present time. With these issues before us, he reviews selected themes from the major educational conferences that preceded the Virginia Beach conference in order to provide the historical context for the current issues. Thereafter, the chapter documents the continued spectacular growth of practitioner-model programs in professional psychology. Implicitly, the data presented in this chapter, especially given the historical context of the present issues confronting our discipline, require us to pause and reflect on the quite extraordinary changes that are taking place. While, for many, the development in professional psychology is exciting, the rapid appearance of so many new and, in some instances, externally unregulated institutions providing education in professional psychology is seen as likely to impact our discipline in ways that are far from clear and far from comforting. At Virginia Beach, one of the tasks was to examine the issues and questions raised by the rapid emergence of professional programs. As Caddy implies in closing his chapter, this task was accomplished within a learning context, in which the conferees were informed about a number of the existing programs and how each was seeking to achieve its educational goals. The Virginia Beach conference was a learning-oriented and consciousness-raising conference. It was not, nor could it be, a problem-solving conference as well. The problems noted at Virginia Beach are issues to be addressed and solved more broadly within psychology as well as the society of which it is a part.

The Virginia Beach Conference on Education in Professional Psychology was a conference whose time had come. So much had occurred in professional psychology since the University of Illinois admitted its first

Doctor of Psychology student in the late 1960s that it is somewhat surprising that this first conference to focus specifically on issues within practitioner-model professional education in clinical psychology had not occurred earlier. By 1978 professional psychology was a reality, but then, as today, the promise of professional psychology notwithstanding, there was a need to examine closely recent developments within psychology and to explore the prospects for the future. While there were many psychologists who were enthusiastic about the emergence of professional psychology, there were also many who recognized the serious need to examine the nature and the impact of the recent growth of professional psychology both on the professional movement and the discipline as a whole. Also, the knowledge that very significant numbers of professional psychologists now were being educated in large programs of unknown quality created the concern within psychology that many poorly trained practitioners might be produced. The appearance of several independent schools of professional psychology in California about the time of the Virginia Beach conference, for example, caused psychologists in that state subsequently to communicate their concern to the American Psychological Association about whether these programs met professional standards (Polonsky, Fox, Wiens, Dixon, Freedman, & Shapiro, 1979).

Apart from concern about the appearance of so many new programs, there was simply a need for communication among the practitioner-model programs about, among other matters, how best to educate professional psychologists. Vexing questions abounded. There were large questions: How can we gauge the public and economic demand for professional psychologists? How will the public view psychology if the discipline permits a continuance of rapid educational expansion without providing clear and definitive control over the educational process? Will professional psychology training programs grow so rapidly as to contribute to the "erosion of excellence" about which Strupp (1976) has reflected such concern? What organizations are most effective for training professional psychologists? How can we assure adequate economic supports for the education and practice of professional psychologists?

There were the smaller, yet equally important questions: How do we select students for careers in professional psychology? What can be done to ensure the participation of adequate numbers of minority trainees in professional programs in psychology? What do professional psychology students need to learn? Who should teach them? And how should they be evaluated? These were but some of the issues which motivated the Virginia Beach conference, which faced the conferees and which continues to face the field today.

It would appear useful at this time to retake perspective on many of the issues facing present day psychology by summarizing the major issues and topics addressed by the educational conference that preceded the Virginia Beach conference. A more detailed historical account of the developments within psychology which formed a context for the Virginia Beach conference is provided by Peterson in chapter 2 on the development of the Doctor of Psychology concept (see also, Caddy, note 1; Hoch, Ross, & Winder, 1966).

The Historical Context of the Conference

Table 1.1 provides a summary of the major topics addressed by the Virginia Beach conference as well as those conferences which preceded it. Analyses of the positions taken and the conclusions reached on the various issues listed in Table 1.1 at each of the conferences prior to Vail reveal only minor differences from one conference to the next, with these differences being accounted for largely by the special focus of each particular conference. By the time of the Vail conference (1973), however, some most significant departures from the traditions of Boulder had taken place and the resolutions of the Vail conferees reflected a number of these changes. These trends may be illustrated by the changing positions taken on several of the major topics by the participants to the various conferences. The issues of social need, research training, and curriculum are representative.

Social Need

At every conference, concern had been expressed about the extent and nature of ongoing social change and the need for psychology to be responsive to these changes. At Boulder (August 1949), the concern was for the need for trained psychologists to meet the increased clinical demands following World War II. The Boulder conferees concluded that there were three primary social needs to be addressed by clinical psychologists: the provision of direct services, the prevention of conditions that require such services, and the enhancement of the concept of positive mental health (Raimy, 1950).

By the time of the Miami conference (1958), there was a marked increase in the promulgation of professional licensing and certification laws, and while the number of psychologists was steadily increasing,

TABLE 1.1 *

Major Issues in Training Treated at Conferences

Conferences	Social Needs [a]	Research	Psychotherapy	Professional versus Scientific	Professional School	Professional degree	Practicum [b]	Practicum agencies	Subdoctoral [c]	Postdoctoral [d]	Graduate Curriculum [e]	Selection [f]	Staff Training	Relations with other professions	Relations with governmental agencies	Controls [g]
Boulder (Raimy, 1950)	X	X	X	X			X	X	X	X	X	X	X	X	X	X
Northwestern (APA, 1952)	X	X	X	X			X	X			X	X		X	X	X
Thayer (Cutts, 1955)		X		X			X		X		X	X	X	X		X
Stanford (Strother, 1955)	X	X	X	X			X	X	X	X	X		X			
Miami (Roe et al., 1959)	X	X			X	X	X	X	X	X	X	X		X	X	X
Greyston (Thompson & Super, 1964)	X	X			X	X	X	X	X	X	X	X	X		X	X
Chicago (Hoch, 1966)	X	X	X	X	X	X	X	X	X	X	X	X		X		
Vail (Korman, 1976)	X	X	X	X	X	X	X	X	X	X		X	X	X	X	X
Virginia Beach (Caddy, et al. in press)	X	X	X	X	X	X	X	X	X		X	X	X	X	X	X

* Reproduced, in part, from Hoch, Ross, & Winder (1966) with permission of the authors and the American Psychological Association.

a Training to meet manpower demands, professional roles, etc.

b Breadth versus intensity, timing, specialty, etc. in both internship and clerkship.

c Psychological technician, expansion of mental health program.

d Requirements, specialties.

e Breadth versus intensity, sequency and integration, core, etc.

f Undergraduate preparation, selection, and recruitment.

g Accreditation, licensing, certification, and ethics.

there continued to be a heavy demand for specialists, especially in the even more rapidly growing mental health service delivery arena (Roe, Gustad, Moore, Ross, & Skodak, 1959).

At the Chicago conference (1965), psychologists in the applied area, in particular, seemed increasingly to be feeling a sense of social commitment. Clinical psychology was seeking greater recognition and was pressing for more and better genuine training in clinical practice. The universities appeared either to be reassessing the present training programs or were actually planning variations, some of which appeared quite radical (Hoch, Ross, & Winder, 1966). Compounding all this was the general personnel resource problem that the Joint Commission on Mental Illness and Health had taken pains to point out and of which the Chicago conferees were acutely aware.

These same themes grew and were responded to at Vail in 1973 (Korman, 1976). By the time of the Vail conference and subsequently, however, the focus regarding the social need had been narrowed and refined to reflect priorities of providing clinical services to those underserved populations that most recently have been identified by the President's Commission on Mental Health (United States, 1978).

Research Training

The so-called "Boulder Model" was designed to produce a scientist-professional who would be trained to be a scientist first and a professional second. According to Raimy (1950), it was this issue rather than any other that created the greatest polarization among the Boulder participants. There were several points that seemed basic to the conflict that this issue provoked: (a) it was felt that students should receive training in both reseach and practice so that they could work on both or either; (b) it was argued that the general lack of dependable knowledge about personality demanded greater research; (c) it was believed that, while it would be difficult to achieve interest and competence in both research and service, the careful selection of high quality students would make such an achievement possible; (d) it was felt that, in the course of the provision of effective services, clinical psychologists would find themselves confronted with significant research problems; and (e) it was believed inevitable that effective service also would provide the basis for much of the clinical research in psychology. By adopting the scientist-professional concept, the Boulder conferees endorsed the basic training model that first had been made explicit in the Shakow Committee Report (Committee on Training in Clinical Psychology, APA, 1947).

At Palo Alto (1955), the decision of the Boulder conferees to attempt to integrate professional and scientific training was reviewed and found almost universal support (Strother, 1956). In fact, the Palo Alto conferees recommended that research training within clinical psychology should be emphasized more than training for service since the techniques and methods being employed within the treatment arena had not been shown to be particularly effective. At Miami, as previously, the conferees continued to define psychology training in terms of the scientist-professional model. The Miami conferees did conclude, however, that research should be defined broadly in terms of a continuum of methodologies and not limited to rigorous hypothesis testing; and some relaxation of the traditional specifications for the doctoral dissertation might be desirable.

Unlike the conferences that had preceded it, the Chicago conference chose to examine the question of training models by presenting four alternative models of doctoral clinical training in the preconference materials (see Zimet & Throne, 1965). In the course of examining these various models two elements became obvious. Firstly, it was noted that the scientist-professional model often had failed to produce a research orientation that graduates of such programs would carry with them in all their professional activities. Secondly, it was noted that many graduates of the traditional model programs did not conduct themselves on the job as scientist professionals but rather as psychotherapists, and that this latter role seemed to meet better the expectations found in the settings in which these clinicians worked. On this same issue, it was noted that many "working clinicians" had expressed concern that their training had not prepared them adequately to function in the roles in which they found themselves. It was within this context that the various proposed models of doctoral training were examined.

The conference addressed the *psychologist-psychotherapist* and the *research-clinician* models in short order. Of the former, the conferees took the position that, in its very narrow conception of the psychologist's role, it seemed to do justice neither to the psychologist nor the setting in which he/she would function. The research-clinician model was rejected for different reasons. In essence, it was rejected because it seemed to add little to the scientist-professional model (except, perhaps, that the emphasis in such a model would be on the scientist rather than the professional aspects of the training). The *professional-psychologist* practitioner model, however, provoked much discussion. Mindful of the problems that had been noted in the traditional training model and of the pressing social need to educate greater numbers of clinical service providers in psychology, the conference did recognize the merits of the professional model and suggested that it may serve well as an additional model within which clinical psychologists might be trained.

In the end, however, the Chicago conferees, like their predecessors, provided their ultimate endorsement for the scientist-professional educational approach. They did feel, however, that the time had come to broaden the scope of clinical training and to diversify training opportunities so that students could build on their various special interests in the course of their professional preparation.

At Vail, the conference specifically endorsed for the first time the professional educational model. And, as Korman (1976) has succinctly stated: "it did so *without* abandoning comprehensive psychological science as the substantive and methodological root of any educational or training enterprise in the field of psychology and *without* depreciating the value of scientist or scientist-professional training programs for certain specific objectives" (p. 19). Unlike participants at any of the previous conferences, the conferees at Vail were cognizant of the reality of professional programming and they recognized also that psychology was ready to support the existence and development of unambiguously professional programs. The outcome at Vail was less a manifesto for change than it was a recognition of what already had occurred.

Curriculum

Until the Vail conference, graduate curricula had followed generally the model proposed by the Shakow Committee (APA, 1947) and recommended at Boulder. This program included two years of study in the areas of general psychology, dynamics of human behavior, related disciplines, diagnostic methods, therapy, and research methods. The internship was offered during the third year and during the fourth year work on the dissertation as well as advanced seminars would be conducted. In the course of exploring curriculum issues at Chicago, the conferees chose not to discuss a course curriculum per se, but rather to specify amounts of knowledge and subject matter that required mastery. A translation of this knowledge into course terms would be left to the university departments.

By the time of the Vail conference there was, as Korman (1976) has noted, a need to build "unambiguously professional programs" in addition to the more traditional varieties. Thus, the Vail conferees recommended that doctoral training programs broaden the range and nature of core academic courses and professional training requirements. Nevertheless, this should be done, it was stated, "without sacrificing standards for educating students in the fundamentals of behavioral science." During the first half of the period between Boulder and Vail, it is possible to characterize the educational developments within psychology as involving growth and expansion yet very limited change. The period after 1965, however, has reflected both an accelerating pattern of expansion and a quite remarkable pattern of change in the direction of professional model training.

Shakow (1978) has commented on the changing view of clinical psychology between Boulder and Vail in the following manner:

> . . . we seem to have developed a more catholic and comprehensive view of clinical psychologists. Not only do they practice within medical settings, which was predominant in the original view, but now they practice in all kinds of social settings and in private practice. They are in tune with developments in other fields, as can be seen in the growth of professional schools, are more in touch with the needs of minority groups (race and sex), both as clients and practitioners, and many practice in a limited way with bachelor's and master's level degrees. In practice, there is a tendency toward a preoccupation with helping people rather than with research and evaluation. Part of this is due to the greater number of persons recruited to the field and the demand for service, but part may be due to change in the structure and goals of training (p. 154).

Recent Developments in Professional Training

But what are the dimensions of the recent changes and the expansion toward practitioner-model educational programming? The magnitude of these changes can be estimated by an examination of the rate of growth of educational programs based on the practitioner-model. Table 1.2 provides a listing by year of commencement of the various practitioner oriented training programs, the degrees offered by these programs and a listing of those institutions in the final phases of introducing such programs.[1]

As is obvious from Table 1.2, there has been a veritable explosion in the development of practitioner-model training programs over the past decade. Whereas in 1968 there were only four practitioner-model psychology training programs, today there are over 30 with another seven or so in the final stages of development. Stricker's (1975) prediction that professional psychology would extend well beyond clinical psychology and into more settings in which appropriate training could be obtained and Cumming's prediction (quoted by Freeman, 1979) that practitioner model programs soon will be producing 95 percent of the graduates in professional psychology both may well be coming true.

TABLE 1.2 [1]

**Practitioner-Model Programs in Professional Psychology Listed by
Year of Commencement with Type of Doctoral Degree(s) Awarded** [2]

Adelphi University, Long Island, N. Y. (PhD, 1951) [a,b,d]
Fuller Theological Seminary, Pasadena, CA (PhD, 1965) [b,d]
United States International University, San Diego, CA (PhD, 1967) [b]
University of Illinois, Champaign-Urbana, IL (PsyD, 1968) [b,d]
California Graduate Institute, Los Angeles, CA (PhD, 1969)
Wright Institute, Berkeley, CA (PhD, 1969) [a]
California School of Professional Psychology, Los Angeles, CA (PhD,
1970) [b,d]
California School of Professional Psychology, Berkeley, CA (PhD,
1970) [b]
Hahnemann Medical College, Philadelphia, PA (PsyD, 1970) [b,d]
Rosemead Graduate School, La Mirada, CA (PhD, 1970; PsyD, 1976) [b]
Baylor University, Waco, TX (PsyD, 1971) [b,d]
Humanistic Psychology Institute, San Francisco, CA (PhD, 1972) [c]
California School of Professional Psychology, San Diego, CA (PhD,
1972) [b]
California School of Professional Psychology, Fresno, CA (PhD, 1973) [b]
Rutgers University, New Brunswick, NJ (PsyD, 1974) [b,d]
The Fielding Institute, Santa Barbara, CA (PhD, 1974) [c]
Psychological Studies Institute, Palo Alto, CA (PhD, 1974)
University of California, Davis, CA (PhD, 1974) [b]
California Institute of Transpersonal Psychology, Menlo Park, CA (PhD,
1975)
Massachusetts School of Professional Psychology, Newton, MA (PsyD,
1976)
Pacific Graduate School of Psychology, Palo Alto, CA (PhD, 1976)
Illinois School of Professional Psychology, Chicago, IL (PsyD, 1976) [c]
University of Denver, Denver, CO (PsyD, 1976) [b,d]
Florida Institute of Technology, Melbourne, FL (PhD, 1977) [b]
Palo Alto School of Professional Psychology, Palo Alto, CA (PhD, 1977)
Central Michigan University, Mt. Pleasant, MI (PsyD, 1977) [b]
Virginia Consortium for Professional Psychology, Norfolk, VA (PsyD,
1978) [b]
South Florida School of Professional Psychology, Miami, FL (PsyD,
1978)

Table 1.2 (Continued)

Synthesis Graduate School, San Francisco, CA (PhD, 1978)
Columbia Pacific University, Mill Valley, CA (PhD, 1978)
Chicago School of Professional Psychology, Chicago, IL (PsyD, 1979)
Wright State University, Dayton, OH (PsyD, 1979) [b]
Oregon Graduate School of Professional Psychology, Portland, OR
     (PsyD, 1979)
California Institute of Asian Studies, San Francisco, CA (PhD, 1979) [c]
Pace University, New York, NY (PsyD, 1979) [b]
Yeshiva University, New York, NY (PsyD, 1979) [b]
New York University, New York, NY (PsyD, 1980) [b]

NOTE. Reproduced with minor additions from Watson, N., Caddy, G. R., Johnson, J. H.,
     & Rimm, D. C. Standards in the education of professional psychologists. *American
     Psychologist,* 1981, *36,* 514-19. With permission of the authors and the American
     Psychological Association.

NOTE. It should be noted that the dates of commencement and the accreditation status of
     the programs in this table relate only to the professional programs offered by these
     various institutions.
     (a) The Adelphi program has functioned with a professional orientation since 1951.
          In 1963 its Institute of Psychological Studies became an autonomous unit of the
          University, and in 1971 the Institute became a Professional School.
     (b) Program in a regionally accredited institution.
     (c) Candidate for regional accreditation.
     (d) Program accredited by the American Psychological Association.

Perhaps the best estimate of the growth (and the possible impact) of
practitioner-model educational programs in psychology can be gauged
from an examination of the numbers of students enrolled in and graduating from these programs. Figures 1.1 and 1.2 provide such data. These
data were obtained from surveying the registration and graduation statistics of each of the currently functioning professional psychology training
programs listed in Table 1.2.

The picture painted by the data presented in Figures 1.1 and 1.2 is
brought into even clearer focus when it is recognized that, during the
1978-79 academic year, the average number of students enrolled in each
of the 37 existing professional training programs was 91. This same figure, calculated across the 107 currently APA accredited clinical programs
during the same year, was 58. Further, during that year, the 20 professional programs that had been in existence long enough to graduate
students at the doctoral level each produced an average of 16 such grad-

FIGURE 1.1

**Number of Students Enrolled in Practitioner-Model Professional Programs
in Psychology from 1964 to 1979**

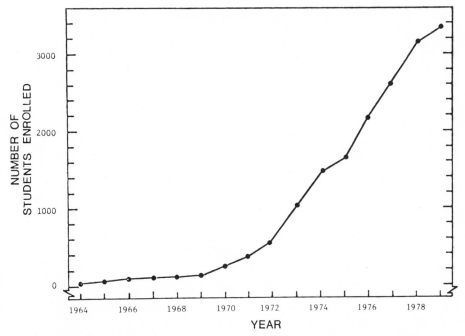

Reprinted with minor additions from Watson, N., Caddy, G.R., Johnson, J.H., and Rimm,
D.C. Standards in the education of professional psychologists. *American Psychologist*,
1981, *36*, 514-19. Reprinted with permission of the authors and the American Psychological
Association.

uates. The same figure calculated for the APA accredited clinical programs in 1978-79 showed the mean number of graduates from these
programs to be 7.6 (APA, note 2).

It is also noteworthy that at the present time there are six programs
which award the Psy.D that have been accredited by APA (University of
Illinois, Clinical, 1970; Rutgers University, Clinical, 1977; Rutgers University, School, 1977; Baylor University, Clinical, 1978; University of
Denver, Clinical, 1979; and Hahnemann Medical College, Clinical,
1979). As can be gleaned from Table 1.2, to date there are three clearly
professionally-oriented programs in psychology awarding the Ph.D. degree that have been accredited by APA (Adelphi, Clinical, 1957; Fuller
Theological Seminary, Clinical, 1974; and California School of Professional Psychology, Los Angeles, Clinical, 1979).

FIGURE 1.2

**Number of Practitioner-Model Programs and Students Graduating
from 1964 to 1979**

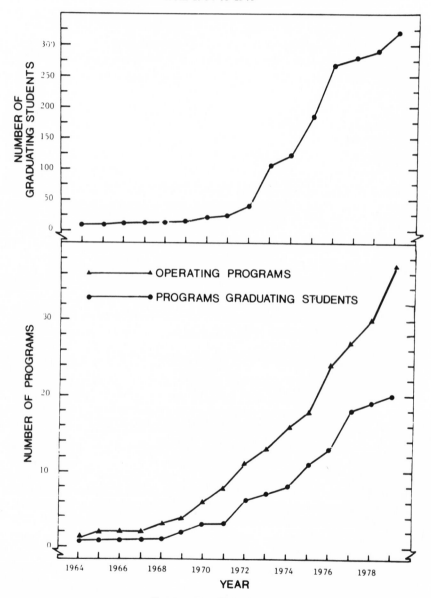

Reprinted with minor additions from Watson, N., Caddy, G.R., Johnson, J.H., and Rimm, D.C. Standards in the education of professional psychologists. *American Psychologist*, 1981, *36*, 514-19. Reprinted with permission of the authors and the American Psychological Association.

The establishment in 1976 of the National Council of Schools of Professional Psychology (NCSPP) provides yet another indication of recent developments within professional training in psychology. The formation of the NCSPP provided an official voice for the professional school movement. Its aims include the gathering and exchanging of information, participation in the development of education and training policy, and providing consultation and fostering research on social problems of human welfare relevant to professional psychology. The council has a four-member executive board that conducts the business of the organization. At the time of the Virginia Beach conference, the council had 25 members. It is anticipated that by the end of 1980 the NCSPP membership will exceed 30 institutions (Zemlick, note 3).

Because so many changes were taking place so rapidly in the educational programming within our discipline, the Virginia Beach conference was seen to have special significance. It provided an opportunity to many of those working within the practitioner-model orientation to gain some most timely perspective from one another regarding what each program was seeking to do, and how each could best achieve the educational goals it had set for itself. It also provided a forum to discuss future directions in the continued emergence of professional psychology, yet it was not, nor could it be, a conference capable of providing solutions to the many issues and problems that were seen to be facing our discipline. The problems noted at Virginia Beach were issues to be addressed more broadly within psychology as well as the society of which it is a part.

Note

1. Virtually all of these programs are in clinical psychology, a reflection of the fact that the development of the practitioner model has taken place primarily within clinical psychology.

Reference Notes

1. Caddy, G. R. *The development and current status of professional psychology.* Manuscript submitted for publication, 1980.
2. American Psychological Association, Office of Accreditation. Personal communication, May 1980.
3. Zemlick, M. H. Personal communication, April 1979.

References

American Psychological Association, Committee on Training in Clinical Psychology. Recommended graduate training program in clinical psychology. *American Psychologist,* 1947, *2,* 539-58.

American Psychological Association, Division of Counseling and Guidance, Committee on Counselor Training. Recommended standards for training of counseling psychologists (Northwestern Conference). *American Psychologist*, 1952, *7*, 175-88.

Cutts, N. E. *School psychologists at mid-century* (Thayer Conference). Washington, D. C.: American Psychological Association, 1955.

Freeman, M. Nick Cummings: Reflections on a controversial past, a full agenda as APA's new president, and a bright future for psychology. *APA Monitor*, January, 1979, pp. 1, 6-7.

Hoch, E. L., Ross, A. O., & Winder, C. L. (Eds.) *Professional preparation of clinical psychologists: Proceedings of the conference on the professional preparation of clinical psychologists meeting at the Center for Continuing Education. Chicago, Illinois, August 27–September 1, 1965*. Washington, D. C.: American Psychological Association, 1966.

Korman, M. (Ed.) *Levels and patterns of professional training in psychology: Conference proceedings, Vail, Colorado, July 25–30, 1973*. Washington, D. C.: American Psychological Association, 1976.

Polonsky, I., Fox, R. E., Wiens, A. N., Dixon, T. R., Freedman, M. B., & Shapiro, D. H. Psychology in action: Models, modes, and standards of professional training. An invited interaction. *American Psychologist*, 1979, *24*, 339-49.

Raimy, V. (Ed.) *Training in clinical psychology* (by the staff of the Conference on Graduate Education in Clinical Psychology held at Boulder, Colorado, August 1949). New York: Prentice-Hall, 1950.

Roe, A., Gustad, J. W., Moore, B. V., Ross, S., & Skodak, M. (Eds.) *Graduate education in psychology* (Miami Conference). Washington, D. C.: American Psychological Association, 1959.

Strother, C. R. (Ed.) *Psychology and mental health.* A report of the Institute on Education and Training for Psychological Contributions to Mental Health, held at Stanford University, August 1955. Washington, D.C.: American Psychological Association, 1956.

Shakow, D. Clinical psychology seen some 50 years later. *American Psychologist*, 1978, *33*, 148-58.

Stricker, G. On professional schools and professional degrees. *American Psychologist*, 1975, *30*, 1062-66.

Strupp, H. H. Clinical psychology, irrationalism, and the erosion of excellence. *American Psychologist*, 1976, *31*, 561-71.

Thompson, A. S., & Super, D. E. (Eds.) *The professional preparation of counseling psychologists.* Report of the 1964 Greyston Conference. New York: Teachers College, Columbia University, 1964.

United States President's Commission on Mental Health. *Report to the President from the President's Commission on Mental Health*. Washington, D.C.: U.S. Government Printing Office, 1978.

Zimet, C. N., & Throne, F. M. Pre-conference materials. *Conference on the professional preparation of clinical psychologists.* Washington, D.C.: American Psychological Association. 1965.

PART B
Development and Basic Issues

CHAPTER 2

Origins and Development of
the Doctor of Psychology Concept

Donald R. Peterson
Rutgers University

To many, Donald Peterson is the dean of professional psychology. In this chapter, Peterson provides his special perspective on the origins of professional psychology and the development of the Doctor of Psychology concept. He points, above all, to the political forces within psychology and beyond, which permitted, resisted, and impelled the development of the practitioner model within professional psychology. It is clear that Peterson is not simply tracing historical events. Rather, he is using the historical context to permit a clearer understanding of current trends in the education of professional psychologists. Perhaps most important of all, this chapter offers Peterson's views on the future prospects for professional psychology as he reflects on professional issues and concerns that we all too frequently have failed to address. In so doing, Peterson does not seek to offer solutions to the difficult issues he raises. Rather, he asks us to contemplate his concerns about the education of professional psychologists. This implicit request was responded to over and over again at the Virginia Beach conference. It is a request that requires attention no less now than it did then.

The first formal proposal for a professional program leading to the Doctor of Psychology degree was made by Loyal Crane in 1925. In an article entitled, "A plea for the training of professional psychologists," he expressed concern about confusions in the training of clinical psychologists. The scientific education and the Ph.D. credential seemed inappropriate for practicing clinicians. People receiving professional services were not clear about the differences between psychiatrists and psychologists. They were either unsure or incorrect in guessing what psychologists were supposed to do. Relations with the medical profession were ill-defined, and when definitions became established they were usually detrimental to psychologists. According to Crane, the main problems arose from the profession of psychology itself rather than from public misperception. The designation "psychologist" lacked social and legal specificity. Anyone who chose to call oneself a psychologist could do so. The Ph.D. degree was no guarantee of professional competence. Because psychology had failed to come to grips with the responsibilities of professional training, the limited prestige accorded psychologists by members of related professions and the general public was sadly justified.

Crane suggested that we put truly "relevant" substance into the training of professional psychologists and use a distinctive degree to certify completion of that training. He proposed a four-year graduate curriculum with heavy emphasis on psychology and those aspects of medicine most pertinent to the study and treatment of psychological problems. He proposed that the Psy.D. degree be awarded upon completion of the program to help bring professional psychology the recognition it deserved and to help clarify the relationship between professional psychology and medicine. In Crane's opinion the public would gratefully benefit from the improved services Doctors of Psychology would bring them.

Soon after Crane made his statement, A. E. Davis issued a comment on the uncertain state of knowledge in early twentieth-century psychology, and stressed the difficulties such limitations entailed for professional applications of psychology. Inevitably, he suggested that a committee be formed to study the various problems involved, and in due time a committee was appointed. The group was chaired by Andrew Brown and included Robert Brotemarkle, Clara Town, and Maud Merrill. Their efforts constituted the first systematic consideration by an officially designated organization of the problems of education for professional service in psychology (Reisman, 1966).

A survey of self-defined "clinical psychologists" working in various professional settings at the time showed that there was little agreement about either the nature of the field or the kinds of preparation required for it. Brown's committee suggested that "clinical psychology" be conceptualized as "that art and technology which deals with the adjustment problems of human beings" and that training be based on a comprehensive knowledge of psychological science ranging from the biophysical bases for human disorder to the sociology required for a grasp of family and community life. At least one year of supervised practical experience was to be required and completion of formal training was to be certified by award of the Ph.D. "or equivalent degree in psychology" from an accredited university (APA Committee on the Training of Clinical Psychologists, 1935).

However contemporary and reasonable these recommendations may sound today, nothing much came of them at the time they were made.

Clinical psychology had not yet established the principles nor developed the methods needed to qualify it as an independent profession. It was functionally ancillary and administratively subordinate to medicine in most of its applications. Clinical psychology did not have the force to be regarded even as a significant upstart by well-established medical professionals. Fernberger's analysis of the composition of the APA in 1928 showed that only 104 doctorally accredited members were primarily engaged in clinical work. The professional activities of these psychologists were restricted mainly to diagnostic testing, under medical supervision.

Even at that early time, a few ideological leaders recognized that medicine was not a suitable base for a profession dealing with human psychological problems. Sigmund Freud (1927) had argued at length that psychology, not medicine, was the basic discipline on which the practice of psychoanalysis should rest. Even earlier, Karl Menninger (1923; cf. Reisman, 1966) had expressed his belief that medicine provided an inadequate foundation for dealing with personal and interpersonal disorders. He realized that preventive efforts as well as remedies were needed, and that the intellectual discipline at the base of professional work should include psychological and social substance as well as biological content.

Neither Freud's argument nor Menninger's was heeded by the politically dominant medical practitioners of the day. Most psychoanalysts came into the profession by way of medicine and managed to define all psychological practitioners who did not possess medical credentials as "laymen." Even Freud failed to grasp the significance of the semantic condition. He presented his arguments concerning the psychological basis for psychoanalytic practice under the self-defeating title, "The Problem of Lay Analysis." Physicians in charge of the rapidly-forming psychoanalytic societies were firmly opposed to Freud's and Menninger's views, and medical training soon was established as a requirement for the fully qualified practice of psychoanalysis.

At the time Crane, Freud, and Menninger presented their proposals, professional psychology was small in size, indefinite in function, uncertain as to usefulness, and unclear about its own identity. Then, and for the two decades to follow, the discipline was too weak to be taken seriously as a profession.[1]

The Boulder Conference

The first strong definition of professional psychology came with the statement of the scientist-practitioner concept by the Conference on the Training of Clinical Psychologists at Boulder, Colorado, in 1949 (Raimy, 1950). By the time of the Boulder conference, professional psychologists had gained recognition for their work in military personnel selection and in dealing with stress casualties during World War II. This new prestige, along with a generous supply of federal money to support the training of clinical psychologists, led to spectacular growth in the field. The number of university-based clinical training programs rose from 22 in 1947 to 42 in 1949. Soon the Division of Clinical Psychology became the largest division of the APA. The critical mass of professional psychologists required for public visibility and political power was suddenly attained. Within a few years, psychology was transformed from a predominantly academic discipline to an organization with a large, vigorous, and often troublesome professional component.

Most of the training programs in clinical psychology conformed closely to the recommendations of the Boulder conference. Clinical psychologists were to be psychologists first and practitioners second. They were to be taught whatever diagnostic and treatment skills were known at the time, but the limitations of available methods were fully acknowledged, and the need for research to develop better procedures was heavily emphasized. Most university faculty members involved in clinical training were far better prepared to teach scientific method than clinical practice, so direct professional training was generally delegated to the medical field agencies where active practitioners and disturbed clients were to be found. In clinical training programs across the country, closely selected young people worked hard and hopefully to become the psychologists their society seemed to need, doing the best they could with the methods already available to them, and at the same time creating better methods through research.

The impact of the Boulder conference, and of the scientist-practitioner concept sanctioned there, was enormous (e.g., Watson, 1953; Reisman, 1966). The profession of clinical psychology was more securely established than it had been before, and the research needed for improving professional service was encouraged. During a period when the technical stock-in-trade of clinical psychology consisted almost entirely of test-based diagnoses and evocative psychotherapies whose weaknesses were even then beginning to show, emphasis on research and development was sorely needed. Even more clearly, affiliation with "science" carried an important political benefit. In moments of candor both psychiatrist and psychologist might admit their uncertainties about the benefits they could offer their clients. But now, when the psychiatrist said, "At least I know medicine," the psychologist could reply, "Well, I know science," and feel at least as secure as his colleague. Psychologists might lose power skirmishes now and then, but their identity was established, and their professional pride could no longer be shaken.

The Boulder Model served its purpose, but also had its limitations as the only pattern for training clinical psychologists. Within a decade, some of the flaws in the concept of scientist-professional programs in academic psychology departments had already begun to show.

The Limitations of the Scientist-Practitioner Concept

One problem with professional programs in academic psychology departments was that they were too small to meet the public need. Size was gauged by the size of other research programs in the department. If efforts were made to expand the professional programs far out of line with other programs, talk would be heard about the professional programs controlling the scientific disciplines and the professional programs would be reduced to manageable proportions. The problem was national in scope, but the effects were most acutely obvious in heavily populated, culturally fluid states with strong research universities, such as California, New York, and Illinois. In the early 1960s, California was becoming the most populous American state. Its public institutions were overburdened and understaffed. A great deal of money had been allocated to the mental health systems, but professionals qualified to operate the state hospitals and other mental health agencies could not be found. The flow of trained clinical psychologists coming from California universities had slowed to a trickle. The University of California at Berkeley was admitting fewer than five students per year. UCLA was doing a little better, but the total annual production of that school was only about 10 students per year. The clinical program at the University of Southern California was administratively disorganized. Stanford had dropped its clinical training program entirely. For practicing professionals feeling the frustrations of a losing battle, but seeing no help on the way, the situation was intolerable.

A second problem with the scientist-practitioner programs was that they offered a poor match with student interests. Few students entered clinical training with strong interests in both research and service. As Thorndike (1955) suggested, and later research (Peterson & Knudson, 1979) confirmed, clinical psychologists tended to be interested in either research or in practice (more commonly in the latter). A single hybrid program, requiring devotion to productive scholarship as well as human service, was ill-suited to their needs. Students interested in practice either had to conceal their intentions throughout graduate study or withdraw from training altogether.

The scientist-practitioner model was aimed at meeting the aims of both scientific inquiry and professional service. In trying to satisfy both aims, it accomplished neither. For all the praise of science students heard in training, few did any research once they became immersed in the demands of professional life. In two surveys (Levy, 1962; Kelly & Goldberg, 1959) the modal number of publications by clinical psychologists was shown to be zero. At the APA convention in Los Angeles in September, 1964, impassioned practitioners seized microphones to shout that they had not been prepared for the demands of professional life. As scientists, the Boulder-style Ph.D.s were unproductive. As professionals, they were incompetent.

Most fundamentally, the academic culture failed to value professional service. The scientist-practitioner programs were located in traditional psychology departments. They were controlled by scholars. Science was glorified. Practice was demeaned. In many departments, the emphasis on research drove professionally inclined students out of the field. At Illinois, for example, over three-fourths of the clinical students entered academic positions upon graduation. A society had been created to train professors to train professors to train professors, while the human problems for which the programs were originally designed went unattended.

The Call for Change

After the explosive APA meeting of 1964, practitioners across the country began to announce that if the universities would not train the professional psychologists society needed, they, the practitioners would. Steps were taken to form a National Council on Graduate Education in Psychology whose main concern would be the training of professional psychologists. The Los Angeles Society of Clinical Psychologists and then other practicing psychologists in California began to organize the California School of Professional Psychology. Similar efforts were undertaken in New York and New Jersey. Throughout the previous year, an APA Committee on the Scientific and Professional Aims of Psychology, with Kenneth E. Clark as chairman, had been meeting to consider the problems scientific and professional training presented to the psychological disciplines. Their preliminary report of September 1964, as well as their final report published three years later (APA, 1967), stated that the Ph.D. programs then in effect for training scientist-practitioners were not preparing either scientists or practitioners very well for the work they needed to do. The report especially stressed that some degree other than the Ph.D., preferably a Doctor of Psychology degree, be awarded upon completion of the program.

The Clark committee report was widely discussed in psychology departments and at state-level training conferences around the country, but the recommendation to develop professional doctoral programs was not generally well received. Psychologists in the state of Washington pondered the problems of professional training at some length, but all they finally proposed were some master's level programs in applied psychology, and even those failed to materialize in the years to follow. A training conference in Ann Arbor, Michigan, denounced the Doctor of Psychology concept and stoutly reaffirmed the scientist-professional model. Only two departments appeared to give the Clark committee proposal the kind of consideration that might lead to the actual formation of professional doctoral programs. In Stillwater, Minnesota, Paul Meehl presented the main arguments for explicit professional training before a conference of psychologists working in academic and professional positions in that state. Meehl later said the conference participants seemed to agree with most of his proposals, but when a vote was called on the actual development of a Doctor of Psychology program in Minnesota, the proposal failed.

At Illinois, Lloyd Humphreys brought the preliminary report of the Clark committee before the psychology department faculty and proposed that Illinois undertake the formation of a Doctor of Psychology program. A formal debate was conducted on the issue and at the end of the debate a standing vote was taken among the 40 faculty members who attended the meeting. A more precise split of opinion could not have occurred. Ten people voted for the proposal, 10 voted against it, and 20 were undecided. This took place in June, 1965, a summer away from the Chicago conference, where the issues of explicit professional training were to receive more searching consideration than they ever had before.

The basic outcomes of the Chicago conference (Hoch, Ross, & Winder, 1966) are well known. Albee's insistence on establishing psychological centers for training psychologists, rather than borrowing the facilities of medicine, education, or some other discipline, was unanimously endorsed and continued effort to form such centers was strongly encouraged by the conference. The need for diversifying the field, and for developing preventive as well as meliorative methods in professional psychology was uniformly acknowledged.

On the issue of outright professional training, however, opinion was still divided. The so-called "professional model" of training, as distinct from the "scientist-professional" model, was debated at length by all the work groups, and several resolutions pertaining to the model were brought before the final plenary assembly for further discussion and vote.

In the end, the concept of the Ph.D.-bearing scientist-professional stood supreme. The principle of training and the essential professional identity expressed in that concept were reaffirmed. A need to experiment with other patterns of training, however, was also generally appreciated, and the members of the conference were willing to wait and see what experimental efforts like the proposed Doctor of Psychology program at Illinois would come to. At the final vote, 12 percent gave "full endorsement" to the training alternative offered by a professional degree program. A larger group, 31 percent, offered "active encouragement" to such a development. The majority, however, 57 percent, were merely willing to extend "recognition" to the idea that explicit professional training programs might be attempted in some university departments, and that the results of those efforts should provide a basis for evaluating the programs at a later time.

However pusillanimous the endorsements of the Chicago conference may have seemed at the time, they at least allowed experimentation with the educational process and offered a willingness to let the results of responsibly conducted training experiments speak for themselves. After further debate in the autumn of 1965, another vote was taken at the university of Illinois to determine whether or not to start a professional program there. This time results were decisive. Full-time faculty voted 3.5 to 1 to go ahead with the program. Three more years of work were needed to gain the approvals, secure the supports, develop the admission procedures, plan the curriculum, and recruit the faculty needed to operate the program. In September 1968, the first class of students began graduate study.

In 1969, the California School of Professional Psychology was incorporated. The founders of the California School decided to award the Ph.D. rather than the Psy.D. because the risks of a new degree along with those of a new organizational form seemed more than could be managed. However, the aims of the school were outspokenly professional, and clearly different from those of traditional, university-based scientist-professional programs. Psy.D. programs were developed at the Hahnemann Medical College in 1970 and at Baylor University in 1971. Then a lull came, until the Vail conference of 1973.

The mood of the Vail assembly was different from that of previous conferences. Important changes had occurred within and beyond psychology. Certainly clinical psychology was a different discipline from that conceived at the Boulder conference. School psychology was assuming a more definite form and higher stature than before. Early methods of assessment, treatment, and re-education had been found wanting, and the assumptions underlying those methods had been questioned. A more mature professional psychology, yielding a few demonstrably effective methods and promising many others, had taken shape. Dissatisfaction with professional training as conducted in traditional Ph.D. programs continued to grow, and the insistence on change was expressed in many ways. The Doctor of Psychology programs at Illinois, Baylor, and the Hahnemann Medical College appeared vigorous and successful. The California School had grown enormously in size and significance. Action to develop professional schools in other states was well advanced. Professional psychology was on the move, and nobody at Vail could ignore it.

Universities had changed too. It was no longer easy for professors to indulge esoteric fancies at the expense of the public and to ignore demands for social benefit from their work. Psychologists with Ph.D.s could no longer be sure of university positions and research opportunities upon graduation. At the same time, the public need for psychological services continued to grow. Mental hospitals were still being staffed by psychiatrically unschooled physicians and inadequately trained psychologists. The need for competent professional psychologists was as great as ever, and sensible forecasts of our social future had to acknowledge a continuing and probably growing need for effective applications of psychology. Programs that offered clear and obvious public benefits received more support than at any time since the early days of the land grant agricultural and technical schools. Psychology, higher education, and the general public all seemed ready for the development of explicitly professional training programs.

The full report of the Vail conference is on record (Korman, 1976). For professional training in general and the Doctor of Psychology concept in particular, two resolutions were especially important.

First, "The development of psychological science has sufficiently matured to justify creation of explicit professional programs, in addition to programs for training scientists and scientist-professionals." Second, "We recommend that completion of doctoral level training in explicitly professional programs be designated by award of the Doctor of Psychology degree and that completion of doctoral level training in programs designed to train scientists or scientist-professionals be designated by award of the Doctor of Philosophy degree. . . . Where primary emphasis in training and function is upon direct delivery of professional services and the evaluation and improvement of those services, the Doctor of Psychology degree is appropriate. Where primary emphasis is upon the development of new knowledge in psychology, the Ph.D. degree is appropriate."

In the year following the Vail conference, activities leading to establishment of the Graduate School of Applied and Professional Psychology at Rutgers—The State University took place in rapid order. For years, an organizing council had been working to develop a school of professional psychology in New Jersey. The group consisted mainly of private practitioners in the state, with help from private citizens who possessed both personal interests in the education of professional psychologists and financial means to help the school get underway. The original hope of the organizing council was to form a freestanding school in the California pattern. The New Jersey Commission of Higher Education, however, had different rules from those in California. The leaders of the council were told that a degree-granting charter would be awarded only if enough capital were amassed to qualify the school as a private college, an amount far in excess of any sum the council seemed able to realize. From the council's side, the search began for a receptive host. From the side of higher education, proposals to develop a school of professional psychology were put forward by the College of Medicine and Dentistry of New Jersey and by Rutgers—The State University. After a round of reviews and hearings, responsibility for establishing the school was assigned to Rutgers.

When the Graduate School of Applied and Professional Psychology admitted its first class of students in September 1974, it became the first clearly identified university-based school of professional psychology in the country.[2] Two Psy.D. programs were created, one in school psychology and the other in clinical psychology. The Ph.D. program in clinical psychology already in operation at Rutgers was continued. However, its purpose, to educate people for research in applied behavioral science, was more clearly defined than before.

Over the next six years, several additional programs leading to the Doctor of Psychology degree were established. During that same time, however, the original Psy.D. program at the University of Illinois was discontinued. In the end, economics and the values of an academic department in an academic graduate college had their way with the Illinois enterprise. The professional psychologists who formed the corps of adjunct faculty essential to the professional identity and effective operation of the program had been hired mainly on federal grant money. When the grants were reduced, the burden of training professional psychologists fell almost entirely upon the full-time faculty members. Faculty at Illinois are selected mainly for scholarly attributes. The dominant criteria for evaluating faculty performance are those of research and scholarship. Given the choice of working with three or four Ph.D. students on one's own research or spending the same amount of time training larger numbers of students in professional skills, most faculty members preferred to work with a younger generation of their own kind. In any case, no more students will be admitted to the University of Illinois Psy.D. program beginning with academic year 1980–81.

As the Illinois program was dissolving, others were forming. Programs leading to the Doctor of Psychology degree have now been established at the University of Denver, The Rosemead Graduate School in California, The Massachusetts School of Professional Psychology, Central Michigan University, The Florida School of Professional Psychology in Miami, The Virginia Consortium for Professional Psychology (College of William and Mary, Eastern Virginia Medical School, and Old Dominion University in association with Norfolk State University), The Chicago School of Professional Psychology, The Oregon Graduate School of Professional Psychology, Wright State University in Ohio, Pace University in New York, and Yeshiva University, also in New York. By now, both the concept of direct professional training and of a professional degree in psychology seem well established.

Each of the programs just named has a history all its own. Every one has required a long time, a great deal of work, extraordinary persistence, and a keen sense of political action on the part of the founders.

Current Trends in the Education of Professional Psychologists

The presently functioning Doctor of Psychology programs differ from one another in many ways. Most conspicuously, they differ in regard to organizational setting. Some are operating as programs within psychology departments, some are established as professional schools within universities or other more general graduate schools, several are freestanding schools, one is in a medical school, and one is in a university-medical school consortium. Each of these programs also differs somewhat from the others in regard to specialty emphasis. Yet, the characteristics common to these programs are far more striking than their differences. Most of them are clearly devoted to the education of clinical or counseling psychologists, but some offer training in other specialties such as school psychology. All of them claim a generic quality that goes beyond clinical psychology, school psychology, or any other special setting and clientele. But there are even greater similarities:

Discipline. All the programs define professional work as the disciplined application of systematic knowledge about psychological process to human problems. Anyone who deals with human problems day by day soon realizes that effective professional action often goes beyond available research. Each problem is different from every other. Complex procedures are designed to suit special problems. This requires ingenuity and creativeness as well as information and order. The demand for ingenuity does not make the professonal an artist; knowledge, intelligence, and discipline are the marks of competent professional service.

Comprehensiveness. In the catalogue of the Rutgers School of Professional Psychology, the term "professional psychologist" is defined as follows:

> A professional psychologist is a member of the organized community of scientific psychology who directs her or his activities towards the task of helping individual, group, or organizational clients with the prevention and remediation of problems in human behavior. . . . The disciplinary basis for modern professional psychology is comprehensive systematic psychology, from biological psychology, through the overt and covert processes of individual psychology, through the interpersonal psychology of small groups, to the structures and processes of social organizations. The parallel range of professional skills includes the assessment and regulation of psychobiological processes, analysis and change of individual behavior and of interpersonal relationships in dyads and larger groups, and the appraisal and planned change of social organizations.

All the other Doctor of Psychology programs appear to be working from similarly comprehensive definitions of the field. Application of so broad a conception means that full-fledged professional psychologists must all understand general psychology very thoroughly, and command an uncommonly wide range of skills in assessment and change. Before a doctorate in professional psychology is awarded, the candidate should know something about biopsychological assessment and the re-education of people with organic dysfunctions, be skilled in the assessment and modification of individual behavior, know how to study and influence interpersonal processes in families and other small groups, be able to examine an organization, know how to help those in control of the organization to make it work better, and be able to conduct program evaluations to determine whether or not change has come about. This is obviously a much more ambitious educational goal than the teaching of psychodiagnostics and psychotherapy, or the psychoeducational assessment and remedial education of individuals. It would be preposterous to claim that every Doctor of Psychology is thoroughly skilled in all available methods of assessment and change over all those levels of functioning. Concentration on individual and interpersonal assessment and intervention is both usual and appropriate. However, the professional programs now in operation seem to demand at least some exposure to available procedures at all levels. This has made the education of professional psychologists far more comprehensive in scope than the professional component of training in scientist-professional Ph.D. programs. It is also more comprehensive than professional training can be in any four- or five-year graduate program that trains people adequately in the skills of research.

Self-renewal. Almost all the Psy.D. programs require a project concerned with the improvement of professional services. The projects differ widely in content. Case studies, literature reviews, theoretical analyses, methodological innovations, new programs, and plans for new programs have been considered in Psy.D. reports. Besides their variation in method and content, the projects undertaken by professional psychologists are usually smaller than Ph.D. theses. Research is not the main aim of professional work and less attention is devoted to it. All of these projects are pertinent to professional service. They witness the need for professional psychologists to evaluate the quality of the work they are doing and to improve it wherever possible. This, as much as any other condition, frees the professional from rigid technical constraints, and promises a self-renewing quality in the professional stock itself.

Unmistakable Professional Identity. The Doctor of Psychology programs are clearly professional. They face outward, toward the public, rather than inward, upon the discipline. Their aim is service, not new knowledge, except for the necessary self-renewal. No pretense of contributory scholarship is made. Mixed and confusing identity labels, such as "scientist-professional," "scholar-professional," and "professional-scientist," are avoided. The culturally established scholar's credential, the Ph.D., is seen as inappropriate to professional function, and impossible to control as a certificate of professional competence. Doctor of Psychology programs are designed for one purpose only: to educate professional psychologists. They use a professional degree, the Doctor of Psychology degree, to certify professional competence in psychology. No doubt can remain about the purpose or content of the programs.

Prospects for the Near Future

It seems likely that many more schools and programs of professional psychology will develop in the years just ahead. Several conditions suggest this. One is the continuing public need for psychological services. American doctoral programs in professional psychology are currently producing about 400 graduates per year to serve over two hundred million people—one-tenth of whom suffer very severe psychological disorders at some time in their lives, and one-quarter of whom probably need psychological services of one kind or another at any given time in their lives. There are some parts of the country where conventional jobs for professional psychologists have become scarce. Clinical psychologists who know only testing and evocative psychotherapy and insist on practicing those skills in Boston or San Francisco may have trouble getting the kinds of jobs they want. But if we are the least bit creative about our services, the gap between what we are doing and what we might do is enormous. We need to go where the problems are rather than where we find living most congenial. We need to attend to people whose needs are great and whom other professions neglect: the mentally retarded, the old, and those in and out of jails and prisons.

There are currently 45 vacant positions for psychologists in the legal-correctional agencies of New Jersey. I know of no organizations in our society more ineffective, destructive, or difficult to change than the legal-correctional systems. Cannot psychologists do some good there if they are appropriately prepared? What about the world of work? It is possible to find ways to make life less miserable on the assembly lines in Detroit, and at the same time save automobile manufacturers millions of dollars each year through reduced alcoholism, absenteeism, and sabotage among workers. What about family counseling? The national divorce rate is climbing toward 50 percent. People considering divorce either want to work things out, in which case they usually need professional help, or they do not, in which case they usually need professional help. Everybody dies. Thanks to Kubler-Ross and others, psychologists now know how to help people face death with more dignity and less pain than before. Why not put that knowledge to better use? It might be possible to overproduce Doctors of Psychology. In fact, the production of too many badly trained, narrowminded, expensive doctoral technicians is a serious danger in our field. However, if we prepare Doctors of Psychology for comprehensive, creative professional service, there is no way to begin satisfying the public need for useful psychological knowledge, let alone oversupplying the need.

A second condition that encourages the formation of professional schools is that they now have some useful services to offer (Peterson, 1976a). If psychology can only offer test-based psychodiagnosis and individual psychotherapy, it is in trouble. By expanding the scope of the professional enterprise from its biological aspect through individual and interpersonal behavior to the psychology of organizational change, however, the list of useful things known is quite impressive. This is not to say that present knowledge and methods should not be improved. More is needed. But documentably useful procedures are available now for improving the quality of psychological life in this troubled world, and professional psychologists are needed to apply many of those procedures.

A third condition likely to lead to the formation of more professional schools in psychology is pressure from students who want to get into the field. Psychology is the most popular undergraduate major in American colleges and universities. Large numbers of students want to enter graduate study and careers in professional psychology. All professional programs receive far more applications than they can accommodate. There is, in one way of looking at it, a very large and lucrative market for the sale of educational and credentialing services in professional psychology.

Coupled with the clamor from students seeking to enter psychological practice is the abundance of practitioner-educators ready to organize professional schools. In a time of limited expansion in higher education, many university psychology faculties see their best hope for new doctoral programs in fields of professional application rather than research. Every large American city contains a community of professional psychologists who would not mind spending some of their time teaching eager young students the skills of helping others, especially if they can be reimbursed for their efforts. If they cannot teach through universities, they are ready to establish freestanding schools on their own.

Along with the sanction of explicit professional training at the Vail conference and the success of most of the programs now in operation, these conditions all converge on the likelihood of more schools and programs in professional psychology in the years ahead. There is no longer much point in asking whether or not to establish more professional programs. The present question is, "How can we educate professional psychologists as effectively as possible?"

Issues in the Education of Professional Psychologists

Several specific questions related to the education of professional psychologists can be identified. These are not rhetorical; they are being answered functionally every day.

How To Gauge the Public and Economic Demand for Professional Services?

I believe that there are no limits in sight on creative applications of psychological knowledge. However, the immediate economic demand for doctoral level professional psychologists is a different matter. We need to explore the fields of service professional psychologists might enter by creative extension of their services. Relevant current needs studies suggest moderate growth in doctoral professional psychology programs, along with clearer definition and expansion of subdoctoral programs to bring specialized services to the public at the lowest possible expense. Firmly based projections of public need and economic demand must be continued as the numbers and size of professional programs grow larger.

How To Select Students for Careers in Profesional Psychology?

Every year admissions committees receive hundreds of applications. From these a few are chosen. How is this done? What characteristics are desired? How are these qualities appraised? Who among us is satisfied with the selection processes as now constructed? How can the processes be expanded? How can it be improved?

What To Teach Professional Psychologists?

Is it reasonable to try to teach professional psychologists the wide-ranging knowledge and the comprehensive array of skills described above? Or is a narrorwer focus desirable? Whatever the content, the educational experiences of professional psychologists must somehow integrate theories, methods, facts, and the skills of application. How can this best be done? Too much didactic material unaccompanied by supervised application is at best boring and at worst conceptually misleading. Disembodied practica (i.e., "experiences" unaccompanied by disciplined knowledge) are either inefficient or dangerous. How can intellectual substance and field experiences be brought together?

Who Should Teach Professional Psychologists?

Academicians, assisted only by working professionals in remote field agencies, cannot conceivably offer the role models, exemplify the experiences, and teach the skills professional psychologists need. The freestanding schools were founded on the premise that professional psychology should be taught by professional psychologists. However, there are also problems with schools run by part-time educators. How can the stability, continuity, and scholarship of a full-time faculty in an academic institution be provided and appropriately combined with the experience, practical wisdom, and professional identity offered by active workers in the field? If university professors spend too much time training professional psychologists and practicing so as to understand what they teach, they may neglect to publish and soon find themselves unemployed. If professional psychologists are brought into universities as full-time faculty members, they become professors. Right then they have lost the professional identity they were hired to provide. The combinations of knowledge, interest, activity, and identity provided by the faculties of professional programs are interesting to compare. Which patterns work best?

How To Evaluate Educational Programs in Professional Psychology?

The problems here are serious ones. The accreditation machinery of APA was built to accommodate small, departmental Ph.D. programs. This agency is now too small and too weak to deal with the growth of professional schools and the other changes now taking place in the education of professional psychologists. Furthermore, the organization may be structurally unsuited to the demand. But what kind of organization can do an appropriate job? How can standards be established for an acceptable program? How can program evaluations be conducted to determine whether or not such standards have been met? How can decisions be enforced once they have been made? One hundred years ago entrepreneurial medical schools were springing up all over the United States. Anywhere a group of practitioners saw a need for more physicians and a lack of educational opportunities, they felt free to organize their own medical schools. At the turn of the century, Illinois alone had 39 such schools. Louisville, Kentucky, had 11. Is psychology today in a similar position? Palo Alto, California, has three brand new schools of professional psychology. Many others are following. How can psychology bring its version of the Flexner Commission into being, and arm it with the power needed to allow only the best professional schools to flourish?

How To Evaluate Professional Competence in Psychology?

The quality of any program rests finally on the quality of its graduates. How can performances be assessed? What is the method for determining who should be disqualified from practice? It is amazing to see how little professional psychologists, experts in the assessment of human behavior, have done in this area. Where should psychology begin? What kinds of credentials should be used to certify professional competence once competence has been demonstrated? In medicine and dentistry, the doctoral degree is the most decisive, publicly acknowledged mark of general professional knowledge. In psychology, an attempt has been made to use the Ph.D. degree for the same purpose, but the use of the Ph.D. as a credential of scholarship over all the arts and sciences prohibits its use as a distinctive sign of professional competence in any one field. The issue is still controversial (Stricker, 1975; Peterson, 1976b). I personally cannot see how we can define content and guarantee quality of education in professional psychology except by using, and controlling stringently, our own professional degree. A doctoral degree, of course, is not enough. How can licensure laws be defined and enforced to make sure that only well qualified people are allowed to practice psychology and at the same time that rights of livelihood and public benefits are well protected? How can continuing education be provided and currency of professional knowledge be assured?

What Organizations Are Most Effective for Training Professional Psychologists?

As well as university-based professional schools and freestanding professional schools, there were three other types of educational organizations represented at this conference. Besides these, there are external degree programs springing up all about us. Still other organizations might be conceived. What structural forms will provide the most dependable supports, the most useful educational experiences, and the most effective quality controls for the education of professional psychologists?

How To Assure Adequate Economic Supports for the Education and Practice of Professional Psychologists?

The importance of these matters cannot be underestimated. Economic conditions have had an important effect on the history of professional psychology. Clinical psychology was practically created by money. It came into being as a publicly noticeable profession largely in response to V.A. and U.S. Public Health Service training funds after the Second World War. The resolutions of the Vail conference were not as closely related to the "maturity of the discipline" as to the economic conditions of the time. The academic market for Ph.D. researchers was weakening. The market for professional psychologists continued to be strong. Garmezy (1978) has forecast a dark future for clinical psychology if federal supports continue to be reduced as severely as they have been over the past few years. However, clinical psychology in 1978 is not the same as clinical psychology in 1948. Reversal of the conditions that once led to growth would not necessarily lead to decline, but the fortunes of professional psychology are closely related to economic influences. How is education to be financed? Beyond graduate study, how are professional psychologists to be paid for the work they do? Many questions about national health insurance, third party payment, and related matters are preoccupying professional psychologists these days. Even tenured professors cannot ignore these issues, for their students' lives, and their own, will be heavily affected by political resolutions to these issues. Psychologists devoted to human service cannot be concerned primarily with their own economic futures, but professional psychologists surely deserve more than the genteel poverty in which members of some other professions are expected to survive. They are not likely to bring their blessings to the public unless they are decently paid, and right now it is not clear how the main patterns of payment are likely to fall.

How To Bring Psychological Knowledge Usefully into the Public Benefit?

Satisfaction of public need is also the final aim of all professions. The well-being of psychologists depends upon their contribution to the well-being of others. If this fact is kept in sight, psychology will be the first profession in history to do so, and many of the other problems will take care of themselves.

Notes

1. The same conditions brought sure failure to the effort to create a Doctor of Psychological Science program at McGill University in the early 1950s.
2. Adelphi University also claims this distinction. The Adelphi program, however, is located in an "Institute of Advanced Psychological Studies." It is designed to educate "scholar-professionals," and it leads to the Ph.D. degree. If these terms are accurate, the Adelphi program is difficult to distinguish from the 101 other APA-approved hybrid Ph.D. programs that offer varying emphases on scholarship and service in clinical psychology, though the place of Adelphi as a pioneer in the education of professional psychologists is secure.

References

American Psychological Association, Section on Clinical Psychology, Committee on the Training of Clinical Psychologists. The definition of clinical psychology and standards of training for clinical psychologists. *Psychological Clinic*, 1935, *23*, 1-8.

American Psychological Association, Commitee on Scientific and Professional Aims of Psychology. The scientific and professional aims of psychology. *American Psychologist*, 1967, *22*, 49-76.

Crane, L. A plea for the training of professional psychologists. *Journal of Abnormal and Social Psychology*, 1925-1926, *20*, 228-33.

Freud, S. *The problem of lay analysis.* New York: Brentano's, 1927.

Garmezy, N. Clinical psychology: Endangered species. *The Clinical Psychologist*, 1978, *38*, 1-5.

Hoch, E. L., Ross, A. O., & Winder, C. L. (Eds.) *Professional preparation of clinical psychologists.* Washington, D.C.: American Psychological Association, 1966.

Kelly, E. L., & Goldberg, L. R. Correlates of later performance and specialization in psychology, a follow-up study of the trainees assessed in the VA Selection Research Project. *Psychological Monographs,* 1959, *73,* No. 12 (Whole No. 482).

Korman, M. (Ed.) *Levels and patterns of professional training in psychology.* Washington, D.C.: American Psychological Association, 1976.

Levy, L. H. The skew in clinical psychology. *American Psychologist,* 1962, *17,* 244-49.

Peterson, D. R. Is psychology a profession? *American Psychologist,* 1976, *31,* 572-81. (a)

Peterson, D. R. Need for the Doctor of Psychology degree in professional psychology. *American Psychologist,* 1976, *31,* 792-98. (b)

Peterson, D. R., & Knudson, R. M. Work preferences of clinical psychologists. *Professional Psychology,* 1979, *10,* 175-82.

Raimy, V. C. (Ed.) *Training in clinical psychology.* Englewood Cliffs, N.J.: Prentice-Hall, 1950.

Reisman, J. M. *The development of clinical psychology.* New York: Appleton-Century-Crofts, 1966.

Rutgers—The State University. *Catalogue of the Graduate School of Applied and Professional Psychology,* 1978.

Stricker, G. On professional schools and professional degrees. *American Psychologist,* 1975, *30,* 1062-66.

Thorndike, R. L. The structure of preferences for psychological activities among psychologists. *American Psychologist,* 1955, *10,* 205-07.

Watson, R. J. A brief history of clinical psychology. *Psychological Bulletin,* 1953, *50,* 321-46.

CHAPTER 3

Entrance Requirements and Assessment of Performance of Psy.D. Students

Donald T. Shannon

University of Illinois, Champaign-Urbana

Practitioner-model education programs in professional psychology have emerged, at least partly, as a reaction to the more traditional scientist and scientist-practitioner programs, which have been seen by some both as unwilling to and incapable of educating psychologists who are especially trained for service delivery. The development of these new programs, however, brings with it a need to explore issues of student selection and assessment. There is reason to question, for example, whether the criteria used in selecting and subsequently evaluating those who are trained as scientists are entirely appropriate to the selection and evaluation of those who will be professional psychologists. In this chapter Dr. Shannon examines the admission criteria and the student evaluation procedures employed in a sampling of the more established practitioner-model programs in professional psychology. The conclusion we must reasonably draw from Shannon's review is that practitioner-model programs are far from achieving a validated, integrated, and widely agreed upon set of selection and evaluation criteria. What is encouraging, however, is the evidence that professional psychology programs are formalizing and advertising their selection and evaluation criteria and that increasingly these criteria are being developed, explored, and evaluated by professional psychologists who are in touch with the real world of professional work.

The rapid growth of professional programs during the last ten years points to the immediate need for responsible, continuing program evaluation to insure quality control of the new professional degree, whether Psy.D. or Ph.D. The relatively large number of students currently being trained in nonuniversity-affiliated professional programs has caused some to fear a glut on the professional job market, and internecine opposition from academically-based, APA-approved Boulder Model programs in clinical psychology. Opposition has always been present, but the "negative attitudes" toward professional programs may be increasing. The 1973 Vail conference, which recommended a clearly professional model of training, has had disappointingly limited impact on the academically-based programs in clinical psychology to date.

Continuing self-examination regarding the quality of admission standards, educational and supervisory practices, and competence of students has consequences for all professional programs, present and future, and societal viability of a separate professional model. As Barron (note 1) expressed it, "Such self-examination has been an important part of our history and involves ethical concerns regarding responsibility and accountability."

Students considering entrance, and even those already in professional training programs, are raising questions of the professional and public credibility of the degrees from professional programs. I believe that those who are on the training end of these programs also must raise these questions for it may soon be necessary to present empirical data to justify the existence of professional programs.

The APA Committee on Standards for Providers of Psychological Services has drafted standards for specialty areas within professional psychology. These standards prescribe the minimal level of training and experience required for professional practice. Despite concerns about quality control in professional programs, the acceptance of professional psychologists as bona fide health care providers has become a reality.

Admission Standards

Admission standards for persons entering professional programs should be based on empirically-demonstrated criteria of ethical, effective performance as professional psychologists. However, such a goal eludes us. Present approximations of relevant criteria are based on limited empirical data and on our collective clinical judgments, influenced by theoretical orientations and clinical experiences. The ideal candidates are the super-bright individuals, whose previous life experiences have enabled them to establish a level of maturity that insures integrity and independence, who have a realistic sense of social responsibility and sensitivity, and who are open to learning and growing from their experiences. Many times, however, pale approximations of this ideal are admitted, using unvalidated other criteria, on the assumption that they will develop into competent clinicians as a function of our training and time.

It is of interest to consider the admission criteria of the professional programs currently in operation. This allows an opportunity to see similarities, differences, and possible implications of current admission procedures across programs. Dana (note 2) provided some comparative descriptive data on the various professional programs operating (or, in some cases, those being proposed) prior to 1977. His report described professional programs or developments at Hahnemann Medical College, the University of Minnesota, Rutgers University, The California School of Professional Psychology, New York University, the University of Illinois, and a humanistic program, the location of which was not mentioned. More recent descriptions from four of the programs described in the Dana report as well as the programs at Adelphi University and Baylor University are presented here. The Humanistic Institute program, the Minnesota program, and the New York University program did not reply to a request for updated information. Table 3.1 presents a broad overview of the criteria currently used in admission decisions in nine programs, including those described by Dana.

By inspection, it is apparent that of the academic criteria, seven of the nine programs use GPAs; five require all three GRE scores; two require two GRE scores; one requires Miller's Analogies Test; one program uses the Strong Vocational Interest Blank; eight mentioned specific background course requirements; six consider previous research experience; five evaluate the quality of previous training background; and five require letters of recommendation.

Regarding experiential criteria: eight consider previous clinical experience; seven require personal interviews; five consider personal life experiences (including autobiographies and other personal data); and six mention other criteria, which include a range from relevant life experiences to conceptual and research interests. Personal characteristics looked at were: warmth, empathy, openness, responsibility, maturity, stability, integrity, imagination, desire for knowledge, and frustration tolerance.

Table 3.2 presents the frequency of evaluation procedures used for admissions in nineteen programs surveyed by Barron (1979). Unfortunately, neither the various programs nor their particular combination of procedures are identifiable as presented, but the university-affiliated programs included those at Wright State University, Rutgers Graduate School of Applied and Professional Psychology, Florida Institute of Technology, University of Denver, Adelphi University, and Rosemead Graduate School of Professional Psychology. Freestanding programs included the Fielding Institute, Long Island School of Professional Psychology, South Florida School of Professional Psychology, CSPP (Berkeley, Los Angeles, San Diego, Fresno), Oregon Graduate School of Professional Psychology, Massachusetts School of Professional Psychology, Illinois School of Professional Psychology, and the Wright Institute

TABLE 3.1

Criteria in Admissions Decisions
Professional Programs

	Adelphi (Ph.D.)	Baylor (Psy.D.)*	CSPP (Ph.D.)*	Hahnemann (Psy.D.)*	Humanistic Psy. Inst. (Ph.D.)	Minn. (Psy.D.)	NYU (Ph.D.)	Rutgers (Psy.D.)	Illinois (Psy.D.)*
Academic Criteria									
1. GPA	X	X	X	X	X			X	X
2. Test Scores									
GRE V	X	X		X	X	X		X	
GRE Q	X	X		X	X	X		X	X
GRE Adv	X		X	X	X	X	X	X	
MAT				X					
Strong VIB						X			
Others						X			
3. Course Background	X	X	X	X	X		X	X	X
4. Research Experience	X	X		X	X		X		X
5. Quality of Training									
Formal									X
Informal	X	X	X	X					
6. Letters of Recommendation	X	X		X				X	X
Experiential Criteria									
7. Clinical Experience	X	X	X	X	X	X		X	
8. Personal Life Experiences including autobiography	X	X	X	X				X	
Other									
9. Personal Interview	X	X	X	X			X	X	X
10. Others, e.g., Career Interests and Goals	X	X	X	X				X	X

* Information updated January, 1980; all other programs' information based on 1978 data.

---

of Los Angeles. Among the preliminary results of Barron's survey of professional schools were the following findings: male admissions (57 percent) to university-affiliated schools are somewhat greater than that for females (43 percent); freestanding schools admit nearly 50 percent each (males, 49 percent; females, 51 percent); percentage of minority

TABLE 3.2

**Criteria in Admission Decisions, 19 Professional Programs,
Barron Survey (1979)**

Procedures	University Affiliated (7)	Freestanding (12)	Totals
Academic Criteria			
1. GPA	1	3	4
2. Test Scores			
GRE	7	3	10
MAT	1	3	4
MMPI/SVIB	1		1
3. Transcripts	4	2	6
4. Writing of Research Sample		1	1
5. Letters of Recommendation	7	2	9
Experiential Criteria			
6. Clinical and/or Therapy Experience	1	2	3
7. Autobiography			
Other			
8. Psychology Checklist		1	1
9. Individual or Group Interview	7	11	18
10. Situation Test		1	1
11. Faculty Interview		1	1

admissions is slightly higher in university-affiliated schools (13 percent) than in freestanding schools (9 percent); in university-affiliated schools, individuals having the bachelor's degree in psychology account for 47 percent of the total admissions, while those holding the master's degree in psychology account for 29 percent of the total admissions; in free-standing schools individuals with the bachelor's degree in psychology account for 37 percent of total admissions, while those holding the master's degree account for 38 percent of admissions. Individuals with degrees in other fields account for 24 percent of total admissions to both university-affiliated and freestanding schools.

Table 3.3 presents the weights assigned to selected criteria by five programs in their admission decisions. Again, on inspection, it appears that personal interviews and GPA are weighted heavily while other criteria are variable across programs.

Details of how the programs evaluate the quality of undergraduate or previous graduate preparation were also requested in my 1978 survey. Replies noted specific required courses. Adelphi expects candidates to have courses in general, abnormal, tests and measurement, developmental, statistics, and experimental. (Students could qualify with reading backgrounds in all but statistics and experimental.) Grades in these courses and the quality of the college are informally considered. Illinois formally evaluates the quality of background training by the Astin Index (Astin, 1971), but particular courses are not specified other than to give credit for a math course beyond college algebra.

The California School of Professional Psychology looks most favorably on students who have done well in classical psychological content areas (physiological, statistics, research design, experimental, history and systems).

Baylor examines the number of courses in psychology taken from departments of psychology and looks for well-rounded backgrounds in general psychology, rather than more applied courses. It also informally weighs the schools attended and grades received. Hahnemann evaluates the content of courses in the applicant's basic psychology background and the quality of the institution attended.

Another question in the 1978 survey had to do with procedures used for evaluating previous clinical experience. The respondent from Adelphi reported that "little data are usually available from previous clinical experiences and so are not significant for most applicants." This view is reflected in the fact that previous experience is ranked ninth among eleven criteria for acceptance. At Illinois previous clinical experience is ranked relatively higher. There, previous clinical experience is rated on a five point scale based upon information from a special clinical experience questionnaire. To receive the highest rating the applicant must have had extensive clinical experience with multiple populations and close supervision, usually from a psychologist with a doctorate; applicants with an average amount of clinical experience in limited settings under supervision receive a rating of "3" and applicants with more limited and restricted contact with clinical populations or social problems receive a

TABLE 3.3
Weighting Assigned Admission Criteria

	Adelphi (Ph.D.)	Baylor * (Psy.D.)	CSPP * (Ph.D.)	Hahnemann * (Psy.D.)	Illinois * (Psy.D.)
Academic Criteria					
1. GPA	2	5	2	2.5	2
2. Test Scores					
GRE V	3	2		2.5	4
GRE Q	5	2		2.5	4
GRE Adv	4			2.5	4
3. Course Background			6	6.5	10
4. Research Experience	8	7		10	6.5
5. Quality of Training					
Formal					11
Informal	7	5	5	6.5	
6. Letters of Recommendation	6	6		6.5	9
Experiential Criteria					
7. Clinical Experience	9	4		2.5	6.5
8. Personal Life Experiences, including autobiography	10	3	1	6.5	
Other					
9. Personal Interview(s)	1	1	3	2.5	1
10. Others, e.g., Career Interests and Goals, Conceptual and/or Research Interests, Honors	11		4	9	8

*Data updated January, 1980

rating of "1." The California School of Professional Psychology looks at volunteer or paid field practice experiences, and requests detailed statements of the tasks performed, the nature of supervision, and the credentials of the supervisors. Baylor views previous clinical experience more as a sign of commitment to the field, and as an estimate of the student's awareness of what is involved in being a clinical psychologist. Hahnemann considers the range of clients, organizational settings, and activities; the amount and quality of supervision; and the quality of the service program.

This survey also requested details of the sort of information looked for in letters of recommendation. Adelphi reported on interest in "freedom from interfering personality difficulties (high anxiety, depression, hostility, manipulativeness, excessive shyness) and evidence that the person has the intellectual abilities, the background of skills, and the motivation for doctoral work." Illinois asks recommenders to provide opinions about the applicant's ability to carry on advanced study, teaching potential, and capacity to pursue a successful career in the field. Greater or lesser weight is placed on the letters of recommendation depending on the known standards, sensitivity, and integrity of the persons writing the letters. The California School of Professional Psychology does not require letters of recommendation. Baylor reported that it has not found recommendation letters very "useful because most are written in glowing terms," but evidence of dependability, efficiency in working, and motivation are looked for. Hahnemann checks for a wide range of characteristics including academic performance, interpersonal skills, commitment to professional work in public service settings, overall maturity and stability, psychological mindedness, self-understanding, and self-acceptance.

Because it was assumed that all programs used a sequential admission process, the survey asked which criteria are used at various stages in screening applicants (e.g., the determination of preliminary cutoffs, further reduction of the pool of applicants, and establishment of the final pool of applicants). Adelphi reported that "general judgment" on the part of from two to four faculty readers serves as the preliminary cutoff. Following this, the pool is further reduced by rating candidates as "outstanding, good, or low probability." The final pool is established by selecting the top 20 percent of the rated candidates for a group interview. In the group interview, 10 to 12 applicants at a time are interviewed by a professor and an advanced graduate student, and then each applicant is rated on a five point scale by each of the two interviewers according "to their promise as a psychologist in the Adelphi Program."

The multistage admission screening and selection process used at Illinois is extremely comprehensive. A complete description of this selection process is sent to everyone at the point of their initial inquiry so that the potential applicant can make a fair estimate of his/her chances of admission. As an indication of the competition involved, data such as mean GPA and GRE scores are provided on applicants recently admitted. Applicants are informed that, in general, persons who have been admitted have GRE scores at, or above, the 90th percentile, and grade points of B+ or better. Also, they are told that their chances for admission are neither enhanced nor hindered by prior graduate study and that previous courses or degrees will not be evaluated until after admission. Table 3.4 shows the Preliminary Admissions Index that is the first step in the admission procedure.

TABLE 3.4

Preliminary Admission Index

		Maximum Points	
GPA (on 5.00 system)	x 700	Maximum Points	3500
GRE (Quant and Adv)	x 2		3200
Astin Score	x 100		700
Math Background			100
Res. Exp. (0 - 5)	x 100		500
Clin. Exp. (0 - 5)	x 100		500
		Total Maximum Points	8500

The last 60 completed semester hours (not including PE, military, or highly specialized courses such as music or religion) are used to compute GPA. GPA is multiplied by a weight of 700 resulting in a maximum possible of 3500 index points. The GRE scores (the typical range is from 1450 to 1600) are multiplied by a weighting of 2 so that GRE usually contribute from 2900-3200 points to the index total. The completion of one math course beyond college algebra receives a weight of 100 points. A 0-5 scale is used for previous research experience (0 = none; 1 = class project; 2 = serving as undergraduate research assistant under a supervisor; 3 = honors or masters thesis or independent study; 4 = junior author on a publication; 5 = senior author on a publication). As described above, clinical experience also is evaluated on a 0-5 scale. Both research and clinical experience ratings are multip'.ed by 100 to arrive at index points.

Next the Clinical Programs Admission Committee, composed of four faculty and four elected graduate students (one from each class year level), selects the top 150 of the completed applications on the basis of the total Preliminary Admission Index (PAI). All minority group applicants, regardless of PAI, are screened by a Special Admissions Committee (composed of minority group faculty and students), who examine each application carefully and make recommendations to the admissions committee. Also, applicants who present arguments that the PAI does not properly reflect their potential due to special circumstances receive special attention from the admissions committee.

At this stage of the admissions process, the letters of reference, the quality of psychological training, the nature and extent of previous research and/or clinical experience, the unique skills or demonstrated abilities, the career interests, and the suitability of career goals and the training opportunities in the program for each applicant are all rated on a five point scale. Based on a rank ordering of the mean of these multiple ratings, the top 50 applicants in this pool are moved on to the next stage.

At this next stage, the top applicants are invited to campus for interviews. At least ten individual interviews (with five students and five faculty) are scheduled so that the applicant can get a good idea of the nature of the program and so that an evaluation of the applicant's "fit" to the program, his/her interpersonal social skills, and the personal adjustment factors needed for the final admissions decision can be made. If an applicant is unable to come to the campus, a field interview with one of the faculty or recent graduates is arranged. This interview is taped for departmental ratings. After the interviewing is completed (usually candidates spend two days on campus), rank orderings are made and used to select the final group to be offered admission.

The California School of Professional Psychology has a different multistage admission process. The preliminary cutoff criteria are GPA, undergraduate experience, and quality of undergraduate program. A reduction of the pool of applicants is based on the autobiography and the applicants' statement of career goals and research interests. The final pool is established by a faculty team that interviews those applicants not eliminated at prior stages of the admissions process.

Baylor reported that all completed applications are randomly assigned to five or six clinical faculty members and that each faculty member recommends up to ten qualified candidates. To further reduce the pool, the folder of each applicant is read by three faculty members who rate the folder on a four point scale. The top 30 candidates are invited for interviews. Each candidate is seen for a 30-45 minute interview by each faculty member and rated. The top ten candidates are selected and offered admission.

At Hahnemann, two faculty members rate completed application folders in terms of four criteria: achievement in psychology, commitment to psychology service, level of conceptual skill, ability to communicate in writing, and level of interpersonal skill. Those applicants who are not eliminated in this process then are interviewed in two individual and one group interview. The average of the individual and group interview ratings establishes the final pool.

In general, schools that have administrative relations with universities admit fewer students each year while the freestanding schools tend to admit larger classes.

Consideration of these admission criteria and specific procedures in general leads to the conclusion that while we are a long way from the unified admission procedures suggested at the Vail conference in 1973 (Korman, 1976), we can detect essential commonalities in admission procedures across programs.

Problems in Admission Standards

A standing joke at Illinois is that admission standards are so rigorous that none of the present training faculty would be admitted to the program. It is obvious that many promising candidates who have the potential and motivation to become effective clinicians are passed over. The current admission criteria of all programs shape and provide the guidelines for applicants to conform to and match in their preparation for graduate study. It will be a wonder if these rigorous criteria do not help spawn a generation of opportunistic "impression managers" whose primary incentive is to "play the game" and do the right things to get admitted to a program, rather than to concentrate on efforts to prepare for carrying professional responsibilities. More and more, young people are all but "burned out" by the time they are admitted to graduate study because they have been concentrating so hard on trying to qualify for admission. Many undergraduate programs seem to be developing the sort of "publish or perish" atmosphere in which graduate academic faculty live. All this happens before they know that being an effective professional psychologist really requires a reasonably put-together human being with integrity, the courage to be oneself, and a model of independence, self-acceptance, intelligence, and sensitivity.

Despite all efforts and procedures, the experience of selecting students for graduate study remains, at least in part, an act of blind faith. We have the GPA, test scores, letters of reference, statements of professed motivation and interest, but we have no adequate way to assess potential to grow and develop as creative clinicians.

Then there is the issue of grades and test scores. Beyond some minimum GPA and GRE scores, there is no evidence that grades and test scores are predictors of success in clinical training programs. Despite the fact that some established programs have completed correlational studies dealing with the relationship between test scores and grades, most programs continue to set increasingly higher cutoff points so that a GPA or GRE that was high enough last year may fall short this year. Grades are not an infallible measure of learning competence or future professional performance. Very high grades more likely indicate ambition, self-discipline, achievement by conformity, and are related to values within a particular college. High test scores often reflect the highest of several attempts at the GRE, or are inflated by special test-taking abilities of the applicants.

Finally, since high grades and high test scores are the common property of many more applicants than can be admitted to professional programs, it is the letters of recommendation, the involvement in research or clinical experiences, and the personal impressions that render an applicant visible to a busy admissions committee. Letters of recommendation, previous performance in clinical experience, and personal characteristics of the individual applicant have become increasingly important.

Assessment of Performance

The problems of assessment of performance of students during their training and in follow-ups in the field are as crucial as the problems of admission. As yet, however, the problems of the process of assessment have been even less systematically studied than those of the admissions process. As a profession, psychology has been struggling with these problems (or perhaps more accurately, has been failing to struggle with them) since the research of Kelly and Fiske in 1951. At the present time, however, clinical judgment continues to be relied on heavily despite the empirical evidence that has challenged the validity of such judgment. There are a variety of issues involved that we must confront.

Recently I have been attempting to construct a questionnaire to assess the effectiveness or competence of the professional work of Psy.D. graduates employed as clinicians. Initially, I developed a questionnaire to be answered by the consumers of the professional services of the Psy.D. graduates as compared with the clients of Ph.D. graduates working in the same or comparable settings. Essentially, I was interested in assessing the effectiveness of professional training programs in preparing students for their professional responsibilities. I included questions about the professional demeanor (likeability and personal credibility), about perceptions of the extent to which the clients' personal difficulties were assessed thoroughly before treatment was begun, and about perceptions of the competency of the clinicians. Further, I attempted to measure the effect of the clinician's degree (Psy.D. or Ph.D.) on these perceptions. I also explored the extent to which the clinician was seen to be effective in helping resolve problems, how empathetic the clinician was, and how knowledgeable he/she was regarding the existence of community services. Unfortunately, I have run headlong into the problem of determining what are reasonable criteria of effective professional competence. Measures of salary, responsibility, and role definition all must be considered and the problems of attendant measurement associated with each must be resolved. It has my head spinning in confusion, but I do intend to focus on these questions or measures of professional competence in the future.

I have identified 32 studies that report information on measures of the competence of therapists. However, it is necessary to define "competence" before it can be measured and as Kiesler (1971) has stated, "If the society of practitioners could specify criteria for effectiveness in an explicit manner, and hand the criteria to researchers as an *a priori* yardstick, then it is likely that institutional research designs could be constructed to answer the question." We are not yet at that point today.

Many of the criteria of professional competence currently being used are confounded with variables unrelated to the training of competent clinicians. For example, in studies using self-reports of consumers, measures of treatment effectiveness very often are confounded with such factors as liking the clinician as a person, or effectiveness being seen as a function of perceived greater similarity between the consumer and clinician's personal, ethnic, or sociocultural backgrounds. Truax and Mitchell (1971), in fact, are of the opinion that no single criterion of client benefit can be expected.

Peer evaluations appear to be the least confounded by variables within a treatment context, but these have not been utilized to assess competence. Professional peers are best able to define what skills are involved in professional competence of clinical activities and services, at least in terms of nonspecifics. (This is the basic assumption and the method used by the American Board of Professional Psychology.) Truax and Mitchell (1971) utilized raters using an "accurate empathy scale" to rate the competence of therapists and showed fair reliability across raters. While this procedure cannot be construed as "peer evaluation" since the raters were "theoretically naive" and the predictive validities of the scale remained unexamined, nevertheless, Truax and Mitchell recommended the use of the scale in a "peer evaluation" context to train clients in the acquisition of interpersonal skills.

Martin (1968) demonstrated that trainees receiving feedback from peer group ratings based on therapy contacts show gains in the area of "accurate empathy," "non-possessive warmth," and "genuineness." Such findings imply that if criteria for effective professional intervention can be isolated, peers may be able to make judgments concerning the "competence" of a clinician, with reasonable accuracy.

Obviously, the tasks of assessment of professional competencies are difficult and complex. The range of theoretical knowledge and proficiencies of clinical skills to be assessed in measuring competence is wide indeed and includes: diagnostic services; treatment of individuals, couples, groups and families; community consultation; crisis intervention; program evaluation; effectiveness as teachers, supervisors, and trainers; and other current professional responsibilities. My inclination at this point is to lean heavily on the use of peer-ratings as the most promising approach to measurement.

In order to be in a better position to assess performance in training, and later in practice, it is going to be necessary to answer hauntingly rigorous questions such as those raised by Paul (1969). To paraphrase: What training procedures? By whom? For which individuals? With which specific training goals? Under which set of circumstances? How does it come about?

Present Assessment Approaches

I asked the six professional programs surveyed to rank-order the criteria used in assessing performance. Table 3.5 presents the information that was returned. Adelphi reported using a pass/fail grading system, with qualitative statements from faculty members for courses and practica. The faculty also evaluates each student twice a year in all activities (courses, clerkships, research, personal attributes, and professional responsibilities) and in relation to personal growth and development in the program. This "progress" report is shared by advisors with the student.

Illinois has an Evaluation and Guidance Committee composed of four faculty and four students who review once a year the progress and performance of each student in the program. As a result, suggestions and feedback are provided, and contracts are established for any outstanding deficits or problems. Each student must select a three-person committee by the end of the first year (two members of which must be program faculty, the third being an outside field consultant) to help plan and monitor his/her individualized program of study. The composition of this committee changes with the development of student's interests and activities. The crux of the entire assessment procedure, however, is the

TABLE 3.5

Weighted Criteria in Assessment of Performance

	Adelphi (Ph.D.)	CSPP * (Ph.D.)	Hahnemann * (Psy.D.)	Illinois * (Psy.D.)
Seminar or Course Grades	2	1	3.5	2
Practicum Grades	2	2	3.5	1
Field Supervisors Evaluations	2	3	3.5	3
Qualifier Examination	—	—	3.5	5
Master's Thesis/Master's Report	—	4	—	6
Internship	4	5	3.5	4
Dissertation/Doctoral Report	5	6	3.5	7
Other	7	7	—	8

* Data updated January, 1980.

evaluation each instructor or supervisor makes at the completion of each training unit in the program. Direct evaluation feedback to each student occurs during and following the masters and doctoral projects, and the qualifying examinations are read and rated by the training faculty with subsequent detailed feedback to the student. Evaluations of performance on field clerkships or internships also are reviewed by the various committees and direct feedback is given to the student. Thus, any individual student in the program is well aware at any given moment of the evaluation of his/her performance by instructors and/or supervisors. "Due process" procedures have been established for dismissing students from the program for failure to perform at an acceptable level in courses or for ethical violations.

The California School of Professional Psychology reported that they use a "global review" of the fitness of each student to continue in their program at the end of the second year. If a student appears to be performing marginally in any area, he/she may be asked to appear for an interview with the faculty. Ten to fifteen percent of students at the school are terminated at the time of their "global review."

At Baylor, the entire clinical faculty evaluates each student's work in courses and practica each year. Feedback is given to each student by his/ her advisor. Qualifying written exams followed by oral exams occur in the third year. Students on internship are evaluated twice by the internship facility and once by a faculty member who visits the internship site during the internship year.

Hahnemann reported that seminar grades, practicum grades, supervisor's evaluations, performance on the qualifying exams, internships, and the dissertation are all equally important in the continuing assessment of students.

One of the recent improvements in the assessment of performance in clinical training activities is that evaluation criteria are now being specified and known by the student. Less specified global assessments and evaluations are disappearing. However, most programs still rely largely on global clinical judgment to assess the current performances and predict the future competence of students. To have any validity, such judgments must be made by clinicians who are in touch with the real world of professional work with human problems, and not by clinically inactive persons cloistered behind the walls of academia.

Reference Notes

Barron, J. A survey of professional schools. Unpublished manuscript prepared for the Subcommittee on Professional Schools, APA Board of Professional Affairs, 1979.

Dana, R. So you want to be a clinical psychologist? Graduate training and informed choice: A student's guide to decision making. Unpublished manuscript available from the author at the Department of Psychology, University of Arkansas, 1977.

References

Astin, A. *Predicting academic performance in college: Selectivity data for 2300 American colleges.* New York, Free Press, 1971.

Kelly, E. L. & Fiske, D. W. *The prediction of performance in clinical psychology.* Ann Arbor: University of Michigan Press, 1951.

Kiesler, D. J. Experimental design in psychotherapy research. In A. E. Bergin, & S. Garfield (Eds.), *Handbook of psychotherapy and behavior change.* New York: John Wiley, 1971.

Korman, E. (Ed.) *Levels and patterns of professional training in psychology.* Conference proceedings, Vail, Colorado, July 25-30, 1973. Washington, D.C.: American Psychological Association, 1976.

Martin, D. B. A method of self-evaluation for counselor education. Bureau of research, Office of Education, DHEW, 1968.

Paul, G. L. Behavior modification research: Design and tactics. In C. M. Franks

(Ed.), *Behavior therapy: Appraisal and status.* New York: McGraw-Hill, 1969.

Truax, C. B. & Mitchell, K. M. Research on certain therapist interpersonal skills in relation to process and outcome. In A. E. Bergin & S. Garfield (Eds.), *Handbook of psychotherapy and behavior change.* New York: John Wiley, 1971.

CHAPTER 4

Professionally-Oriented Training and the Baylor Response

Mac Sterling
Baylor University

The Baylor University Department of Psychology has had almost a decade to de-velop a strong and well integrated Doctor of Psychology program. By 1980, the Baylor program had graduated a total of 75 professional psychologists, with an average of about 10 per year over the past five years. In this chapter, Dr. Sterling presents the basic philosophical assumptions on which the Baylor program is based, and he outlines the curriculum which illustrates both the breadth of, and the pri-orities within, the Baylor program. This chapter is significant, not because the Baylor program is unique, but because it describes a firmly established and rigorous practitioner-model program in professional psychology that has run smoothly within a university-based department of psychology for a decade.

Ever since 1898, when Lightner Witmer pleaded with his colleagues to define clinical psychology and to train students in a manner that was appropriate for the task they would be doing as professionals, there has been a continuous group of individuals echoing a similar concern. In recent years, groups such as the Subcommittee of 50 of the Education and Training Board of the American Psychological Association (APA), the National Council on Graduate Education in Psychology, and the Division of Psychotherapy of the APA have renewed the cry. Often these suggestions have fallen on deaf ears, but slowly there have been some changes. Many of the clinicians were in agreement, but the impediment to change was in the implementation. Universities have been slow to change. Some have been reluctant and looked the other way in hopes that the clinicians would go away, or be absorbed by another discipline and leave psychology alone to become a pure science. Throughout this process of clinical psychology's evolution there have been several perennial suggestions advanced. In this chapter I would like briefly to review these issues and a few concerns of which I have been particularly aware. Then, I would like to show how we at Baylor have attempted to design a curriculum and a program to solve some of these problems, which I consider inherent in the education and training of clinical psychologists.

One of the continuing suggestions offered to universities is that clinical graduate programs should combine practice with theory and these experiences should run concurrently where possible. Furthermore, equal time should be given to the practice of psychology and research practice. Clinical students should be given enough qualified training to be able to function in diagnosis and therapy at a journeyman level.

Another recurring concern has centered on clinical psychologists being viewed as legitimate first-class members of psychology. For example, it has been recommended that the director of the clinical program should be ranked equally with the other faculty members of the department and should be included in the tenure tract. The clinical faculty should be given time in the teaching load to implement the necessary training. In addition, most of the committees on training have emphasized strongly that the clinical faculty should be practicing clinicians, as well as researchers and teachers, to act as role models.

A third recommendation relates to the need for the university to be cognizant of the people whom they select for training. The students should be people who have the interpersonal skills to relate to and instill trust in others. They should be individuals who are mature, responsible, and trained to function as scholars as well as to deliver caring mental health services. For the university to accomplish this personal dimension in training, there needs to be an atmosphere in the training program conducive to personal growth and development.

A fourth suggestion discussed has been the need for clinical psychology to be desirous of social betterment and to assist the minority sector to make use of the mental health services available. This will require the development of new techniques and procedures adapted for those individuals who are unable to respond to or perhaps assess the private practice model.

Finally, clinical psychology has been called on to meet an ever-expanding role in social planning and administration. Thus, the private practice model is not sufficient for much of the clinician's work. The training should be broadened to include role definitions and skills necessary to function in social welfare agencies and as mental health consultants in other diverse situations.

We at Baylor have agreed with these concerns through the years and have attempted to design our program to implement these changes. Between the years of 1958 and 1966, Baylor had a small, traditional Ph.D. clinical program that we discontinued because there were not enough adjunct clinicians in the community at that time to provide quality practica supervision. However, we gained a considerable amount of knowledge about the problems of graduate education from this program. In 1971, when we felt that adequate resources were available to permit the development of a successful Psy.D. program, we attempted to incorporate these ideas into our model.

The basic premises we derived from our earlier experience are as follows:

- Our basic philosophy is that the Ph.D. and Psy.D. are complementary and that both have a vital role in the training of clinical psychologists. Our discipline needs a solid base of knowledge derived from research. Those individuals who want to specialize in the research arm of clinical psychology should receive a Ph.D. and be well trained in research methodology. The Psy.D. or professional school training is for those individuals who want to tip the balance of their activity toward the applied area. Most training programs have not been able to accomplish both functions within a reasonable time, and most students have not been able to become equally successful in both areas.
- In the past, both students and faculty were expected to be experts in everything. The actual facts suggest there are individual differences between both groups. Some are more interested in and capable of practice than research and vice versa. However, the programs have made the student interested in applied work wait until the internship year to learn the applied skills.
- A dissertation is practice in research for those who will be doing that as their life's work. Clinical practicum training is practice in clinical functioning for those who will be doing that as their life's work.
- Clinical training programs are often very expensive and inefficient for both the university and the student. This seems to be, at least in part, due to the fact that the student enters graduate training on an individual tract. Because the student proceeds individually, there are often semesters when the student does not take courses or move along because he or she is attempting to decide on a dissertation topic or studying for qualifying exams. These delays add months and years to the program. The students' incomes are delayed, and they are an expense to the university because of assistantships and stipends that could be used for other students. Another expensive procedure is the process of sending the student off on internship and then having him or her return to finish the dissertation. Many of these students never finish their doctorates once they leave the university.
- Clinical judgment and confidence develop from the volume and vari-

ety of clinical exposure, the transfer of training between material learned in the classroom and that applied to actual living problems, and the sense of realism that develops when there is built into the experience the possibility of seeing the consequences of recommendations and judgments.

- Learning takes place best when the situation is nonthreatening and emphasis is on self-growth. To accomplish this, the students should be encouraged to cooperate rather than compete. They should be helped to see that the real adversaries they are to master are the problems they will encounter in their practice, and not each other. Learning is also enhanced when the curriculum involves the student immediately at the individual interest level and does not delay personal involvement for a year or so. Frequent feedback of the student's progress further enhances growth and the shaping of effective clinical skills.
- Finally, careful attention should be given to selection but once the selection is made, every effort should be exerted to help the student become the unique individual he or she is capable of being. A close personal, helping relationship between student and faculty seems the mode to attend to this vital dimension.

Baylor is a medium-sized university located halfway between Dallas and Austin. It emphasizes undergraduate teaching and community service. The psychology department has stayed within this medium size also. There are presently a total of 32 graduate clinical students on campus, with 10 away on internship. There are 6 full-time clinical faculty and approximately 20 associate clinical faculty in the practicum agencies. The ratio of students to faculty ranges between 5 and 6 to 1. All of the clinical faculty were recruited to represent different theoretical viewpoints. Also, all the faculty are in the tenure tract.

The program is four years long, including summers. Ten students are admitted each fall as a class and they take all their classes together, with the exception of practicum courses and individualized personal development. Most of the courses, especially skill courses, are restricted to Psy.D. students so that the enrollment in each course is 10. During these four years there are 98 semester hours of course work.

All students are placed in practicum training from the beginning of the program. Each student works from 16 to 20 hours per week in addition to taking a full academic load. This means that each student accumulates 2600 to 3000 hours of supervised clinical experience before the internship. Every effort is made to place students in settings appropriate to their capabilities. Furthermore, we believe that a student learns best when immersed in a clinical setting and so we have avoided having a special clinic on campus. Students are sent into the community (usually

10 different agencies) where they learn to function within the total context and with a variety of professionals and paraprofessionals. Full-time clinical faculty serve as consultants to practicum agencies, many of which do not have full-time psychologists. These faculty function as role models as well as practicing clinicians.

The courses for the first year are as follows:

FALL	SEMESTER HOURS
Learning	3
Psychological Assessment (Intellectual)	4
Counseling Psychology	3

We immediately give the students a skill course in intellectual assessment so that they can function better in the practicum agencies and can make better use of their experience. This course in intelligence testing introduces them to the process of traditional psychodiagnostics. Much of the clinicians' work involves this function because there is still a great need in the mental health field for good diagnosticians.

SPRING	SEMESTER HOURS
Community Mental Health	3
Advanced Psychopathology	3
Developmental Psychology	3

During the spring of the first year, the students are exposed to more of the basic areas underlying clinical psychology. The emphasis is not only on practical knowledge of these areas, but on the research findings as well.

SUMMER	SEMESTER HOURS
Clinical Psychology	3
Human Information Processing	3
Individualized Professional Development	3

The students become well steeped in the professional issues and ethics in the course in Clinical Psychology. Also, there is the second course in a more basic area of psychology, Individualized Professional Development. The students select areas where they feel the need for extra assistance, such as more supervision in a therapy class. The students may bring in videotapes and will review these tapes with the professor. However, this course cannot be used for psychotherapy for the student's personal life.

SECOND YEAR

FALL	SEMESTER HOURS
Psychological Assessment (Personality)	4
Behavior Therapy	3
Social Psychology and Group Dynamics	4
Clinical Practicum	3

During the second year, the students are encouraged to sharpen diagnostic skills. The courses in assessment, with strong emphasis on projectives and behavior therapy, prepare them to broaden their functioning in the practicum agency. The course in group dynamics is didactic preparation for the experience they will encounter in the spring as a member of a group and as they begin to function as group therapists in the practicum agencies.

SPRING	SEMESTER HOURS
Theories	3
Group Psychotherapy	4
Clinical Practicum	3

The emphasis in the spring is to supplement the psychodiagnostic development with psychotherapy training. In the course in psychotherapy, they try out various therapy techniques through role play. In the group therapy course, the class of 10 functions as a group and is led by a clinical associate, not involved in evaluation, to experience the process of group therapy.

SUMMER	SEMESTER HOURS
Personality	3
Psychotherapy Procedures with Children	3
Individual Project in Clinical Psychology	3
Clinical Practicum	3

Most of the students have good undergraduate training in personality theory. At this time in their program, they are encouraged to critically evaluate and relate the theories with the new information gained from their practice and study during the past two years. They are helped to conceptualize and integrate the theories into a workable and meaningful system for themselves. Family therapy is emphasized in the Psychotherapy Procedures with Children course, but there is also exposure to the unique problems of children.

THIRD YEAR

FALL	SEMESTER HOURS
Introduction to Experimental Design	4
Community Psychology	3
Neuropsychology and Neuropharmacology	3
Clinical Practicum	3

Students take preliminary exams and oral exams in the fall of the third year and begin to make contact with internship agencies for possible placement. This is also the year of refinement in clinical knowledge and skills. Experimental design helps to more firmly anchor the students in general psychology and make them better consumers of research.

SPRING	SEMESTER HOURS
Medical Psychology	3
Psychophysiology and Biofeedback	3
Clinical Practicum	3

During this semester, the refinement continues. A practicing psychiatrist from the community teaches the Medical Psychology course with special emphasis on the medical orientation. This is felt to be quite valuable since many of the graduates work in medical schools or in settings where there is a strong medical influence. Psychophysiology is the last of the general psychology courses. It is presented at a time when it can be correlated with the knowledge being learned in Medical Psychology.

SUMMER	SEMESTER HOURS
Individual Project in Clinical Psychology	3
Case Studies	3
Clinical Practicum	3

This summer is spent in finalizing a special project paper begun the previous summer and in presenting it to graduate students and faculty. In the Case Studies course, special problems from the agencies are brought in for analysis and the clinical associates sit in to share perspectives. This is a period of final integration and summing up before leaving for internship.

FOURTH YEAR

Twelve Month Internship   3 Semester Hours

The internship is seen as part of the educational process, where the final honing of clinical skills is accomplished. Each student individually contacts and negotiates with the facility of his or her choice. Final approval of the practicum facility is given by the clinical faculty. The internship must involve a rotation through more than one experience and should involve a variety of doctoral level psychologists as supervisors. Proposed internship placements such as with private practitioners or hospitals with only one service to be filled are not usually approved.

The students are encouraged to take an internship away from the university and the local community. In fact, they are restricted from taking an internship in an agency where they formerly have been assigned a practicum. Upon satisfactory completion of the internship, they are finished with work at the university, and may or may not return for graduation.

Baylor maintains a close relationship with the internship facility during the year. An evaluation of each student is sent to the university in midyear and at the completion of the program. In the spring of each year, each internship facility is visited by a member of the clinical faculty as a way of maintaining a liaison with the facility and to evaluate it as a training facility for future students. Upon receiving certification of successful completion of the internship, the student receives the Psy.D. degree at graduation in August, four years after he or she began.

CHAPTER 5

Planning Practicum Programs Within Professional Psychology Training: A Systems Approach

Daniel B. Fishman
Rutgers University

The most significant components within practitioner-model programs in professional psychology that discriminate them from the more traditional scientist-practitioner training programs are those involving the provision of practicum training. In this chapter, Dr. Fishman provides an account of a systems approach to practicum training that offers a particularly appropriate model for the development of integrated high-quality practicum training within a professional program. This chapter is especially important because the model presented represents an exception in practicum educational efforts for it permits both the integration and the diversification of theoretical and practical learning that is essential to quality practicum education in professional psychology. Further, the chapter offers a description of and the rationale for what Fishman considers to be the most viable solution to the problems of bringing together the academic and public practitioner cultures for the appropriate training of professional psychologists. This new system he describes as the Integrated Service Center. While such centers are only in the early stages of development, Fishman may well be right when he asserts their special value in the education of professional psychologists. As this chapter describes, this approach has been operationalized and it can be tested for its contribution both to the provision of community services and the education of professional psychologists.

The 1973 Vail Conference on Level and Patterns of Professional Training in Psychology (Korman, 1976) articulated an innovative and increasingly accepted model of professional training. Several of the conference's recommendations are particularly relevant to the development of practicum components in such training. These include:

- A professional psychology training program "shall include a significant proportion of field (practicum) experience at all training levels, and field experiences shall be integrated with theoretical and didactic education throughout the course of study" (p. 100);

65

- In comparison to previous types of practicum training, "the content of professional experiences (should) be diversified and broadened to incorporate the development of a variety of specific job skills not traditionally included in doctoral training programs, such as administrative skills, program development and evaluation, and field research" (p. 103);
- "In courses devoted to training in professional skills, more attention should be given to practicum experience in diverse community and institutional settings" (p. 118); and
- "Training programs must be oriented towards training people to work in human service centers, broadly conceived" (p. 118).

Using the above recommendations as guidelines, and taking a systems analytic approach to professional training as a whole, the faculty members at the Rutgers Graduate School of Applied and Professional Psychology have developed a conceptual model of professional psychology training.

The model begins with the goal of training professional psychologists to function within an integrated human service delivery system. This integrated system includes the whole network of programs (e.g., physical health, mental health, welfare, education, rehabilitation, corrections, job training, housing, and food) that help people lead more comfortable, happy, and productive lives, and aid society constructively to solve its social problems.

The emphasis upon integrating human services is important because people's service needs are usually interrelated and services should be defined for people's problems. For example, physical illness can precipitate depression. On the other hand, depression can be manifested in physical symptoms. Some other examples: mental health consultation can help industrial productivity; poverty can exacerbate family tensions; and childhood emotional problems can interfere with proper education. Since mental health needs are embedded in a total life context, we believe that professional psychologists must be able to deliver services in a manner that takes into account and mobilizes all relevant human services.

For any particular conceptual perspective (such as that of providing outpatient therapy), the roles and associated competencies of professional psychologists should be articulated and differentiated from the roles of other professionals and paraprofessionals. These competencies are clustered into degree programs, and curricula are designed to train these competencies. Criteria and methods are developed to evaluate whether the training results in the desired competencies.

The roles and competencies of psychologists must be elaborated from a variety of conceptual perspectives that relate to the human service

FIGURE 5.1

Nine Conceptual Perspectives for Viewing Human Service Transactions

*EXPLANATORY NOTE: Within the oval, the basic structure of a Human Service Transaction is presented, consisting of a Service Provider engaging in a Service Activity to help a Service Recipient. Outside the oval are nine different conceptual perspectives for viewing the Human Service Transaction. The dashed lines indicate the particular component of the transaction that the perspective illuminates. Generally, the perspectives fall into three clusters: Perspectives 1-4 focus on the specific content of the service; Perspectives 5 and 6, on the theory underlying the service; and Perspectives 7-9, on the process by which the service is delivered.

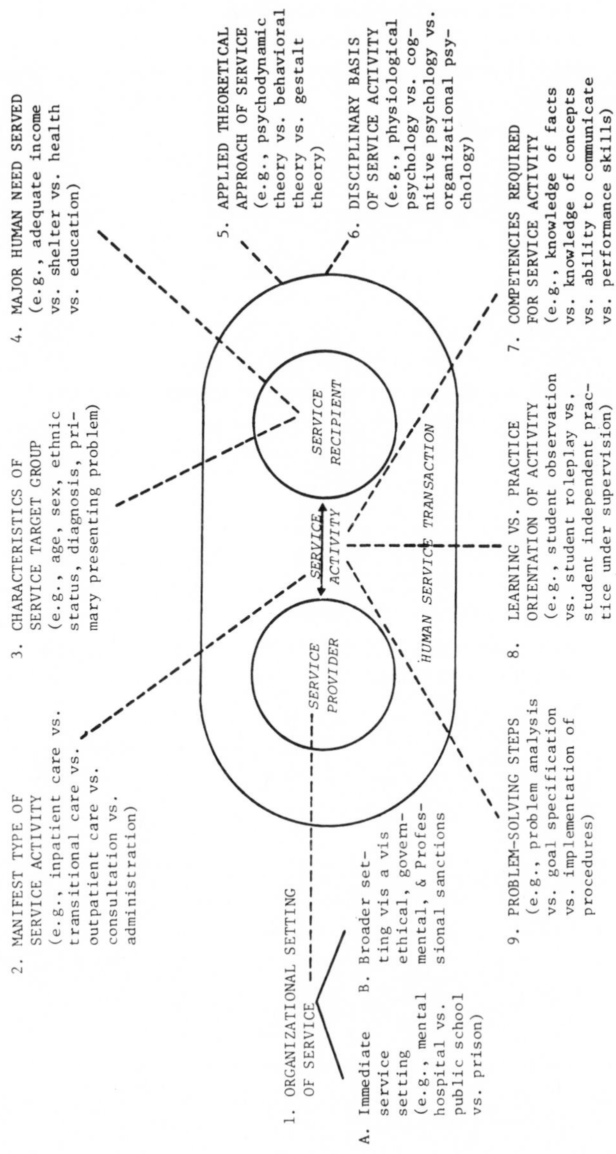
1. ORGANIZATIONAL SETTING OF SERVICE
A. Immediate service setting (e.g., mental hospital vs. public school vs. prison)
B. Broader setting vis a vis ethical, governmental, & Professional sanctions
2. MANIFEST TYPE OF SERVICE ACTIVITY (e.g., inpatient care vs. transitional care vs. outpatient care vs. consultation vs. administration)
3. CHARACTERISTICS OF SERVICE TARGET GROUP (e.g., age, sex, ethnic status, diagnosis, primary presenting problem)
4. MAJOR HUMAN NEED SERVED (e.g., adequate income vs. shelter vs. health vs. education)
5. APPLIED THEORETICAL APPROACH OF SERVICE (e.g., psychodynamic theory vs. behavioral theory vs. gestalt theory)
6. DISCIPLINARY BASIS OF SERVICE ACTIVITY (e.g., physiological psychology vs. cognitive psychology vs. organizational psychology)
7. COMPETENCIES REQUIRED FOR SERVICE ACTIVITY (e.g., knowledge of facts vs. knowledge of concepts vs. ability to communicate vs. performance skills)
8. LEARNING VS. PRACTICE ORIENTATION OF ACTIVITY (e.g., student observation vs. student roleplay vs. student independent practice under supervision)
9. PROBLEM-SOLVING STEPS (e.g., problem analysis vs. goal specification vs. implementation of procedures)
SERVICE PROVIDER
SERVICE ACTIVITY
SERVICE RECIPIENT
HUMAN SERVICE TRANSACTION

transaction between the service provider and the service recipient. Nine such perspectives are outlined in Figure 5.1. These perspectives fall into several clusters:

• The specific content of the service, including its organizational setting, whether it involves inpatient, outpatient, or other modalities of care, characteristics of the service target group, and the major human need being served;
• The psychological theory underlying the service; and
• The process by which the services are delivered.

At Rutgers we have used the outline in Figure 5.1 to develop a questionnaire, called QUEST, to describe systematically and comprehensively the content of any course of practicum experience in a professional psychology training program. The form elaborates each conceptual perspective into one or more variables, and each variable is in turn divided into an exhaustive set of mutually exclusive categories for describing the course or practicum experience. We are using the form to collect student and faculty perceptions of the courses and practicum experiences that are offered in the curriculum.

A sample page from the QUEST form is shown in Figure 5.2. It lists the categories associated with the perspective, learning versus practice orientation of service activity (cf. Figure 5.1, perspective 8). A course is described in terms of this perspective by rating each category according to the degree that it is relatively emphasized, from "3-Strong emphasis," to "0-None."

Planning and Implementing Practicum Training

The learning versus practice perspective listed in Figure 5.2 relates directly to an important issue in practicum training. There is a continuum of increasing independent involvement in the role of service practitioner that ranges from listening to didactic material and observing practice to independent service provision.

Traditionally, the curriculum in applied psychology training has been divided into two discrete parts: theoretical, classroom work, dealing with the earlier steps in the learning-versus-practice continuum; and practicum training, dealing with the later steps. However, this arrangement frequently leads to a lack of integration between the steps. Thus, students often will remark that "being out in the real world" of a practicum agency is miles apart from "all the theory" taught in the classroom. What is reflected in such remarks is a troublesome discrepancy between the culture of the university and the culture of the public service agency.

At Rutgers the curriculum is organized so that theoretical, didactic training is not the exclusive province of the university classroom; and applied, practicum training, the exclusive province of the nonuniversity

FIGURE 5.2

Sample Page from the "QUEST" Form

Conceptual Perspective/ Variable	Category	Relative Emphasis of Category in Course: 3=Strong, 2=Moderate, 1=Limited, 0=None
8. Learning vs Practice Orientation of Service Activity*	1. Student <u>listening</u> to didactic lecture: <u>theory</u>-oriented . .	_____
	2. Student <u>listening</u> to didactic lecture: <u>case</u>-oriented . . .	_____
*NOTE: "Service Activity" refers to both "treatment" and "support" activities, as listed on page 4 of this form.	3. Student <u>reading</u> didactic Material: <u>theory</u>-oriented . . .	_____
	4. Student <u>reading</u> didactic material: <u>case</u>-oriented	_____
	5. Student <u>discussing</u> didactic material: <u>theory</u>-oriented .	_____
	6. Student <u>discussing</u> didactic material: <u>case</u>-oriented . .	_____
	7. Student <u>observing</u> practice of a performance skill	_____
	8. Student <u>roleplaying</u> a client.	_____
	9. Student <u>roleplaying</u> a help-giver role (frequently involving skills in #7)	_____
	10. Student <u>participating</u> in client role (e.g., T-Group) . .	_____
	11. Student <u>acting as co-clinician</u> together with an experienced clinician	_____
	12. Student independently <u>providing service</u> under simultaneous supervision (one-way mirror or simultaneous television)	_____
	13. Student independently <u>providing service</u> under non-simultaneous supervision	_____
	14. Student independently <u>providing service</u> without specific supervision	_____
	97. Other than Categories 1-96 (describe)	_____
	98. Categories 1-97 Not Applicable	_____

service agency. Several examples illustrate how this is accomplished. In a course on introduction to psychodynamic interviewing, theoretical material is read and discussed, the students observe the course instructor conduct a model interview with an actual client, and each student conducts an interview with an actual client while being observed by the whole class. In a course on adult psychopathology, about half the sessions involve visits to local psychiatric hospitals and correctional institutions, in which the instructor or one of the students interviews a patient who illustrates a certain type of psychopathology. In a course on program evaluation, part of the student's work consists of conducting a real program evaluation study in an outside service agency. In a course on community psychology, part of the student's work involves an apprenticeship with a community psychologist in an outside service agency.

Didactic training also is used to supplement practicum experiences. All clinical students take two semesters of a course called Advanced Practicum Supervision, in which they present, review, and analyze issues that arise directly out of their ongoing practicum placements. In a course on Professional Development, which deals with ethical, professional, judicial, and legislative factors in practice, an important focus is to relate these factors to the students' experiences in their ongoing practicum placements. For some practicum placements, individual supervision by the agency itself is supplemented with individual supervision by faculty at the university. In a number of applied courses, such as the Psychodynamic Treatment of Adolescents, the student is required to have one or more ongoing therapy cases that are treated within the theoretical and procedural framework of the course; these cases are seen as part of the student's practicum setting.

The Structure of Practicum Training

The present practicum training in the clinical program at Rutgers has a number of important objectives: (a) to provide students with educationally meaningful service roles; (b) to provide high quality supervision of student clinical activities; (c) to expose students to a broad spectrum of types of clients, types of services, and types of human service organizations; and (d) to generate stipends to help meet students' financial needs.

To attain these objectives, the practicum training program is structured into four basic elements: (a) ongoing placement in outside practicum agencies, for one or two days a week, during the first three years of training; (b) carrying a minimum of two cases over a full academic year in the school's psychological clinic; (c) spending the fourth year in a fulltime clinical internship; and (d) applied experiences in didactic classes, such as the observation of faculty clinical activities. This arrangement seems to be a definite improvement over traditional "Boulder Model" clinical Ph.D. programs. However, there are still disturbing structural problems that also pervade medical, legal, and other professional training.

These problems revolve around the conflicts between the academic culture of the university, and the practitioner culture of the public service agency (the primary organizational setting for which we are training our students). As is widely known, there are different incentives and resultant priorities in each of these two cultures. For example, an important incentive for the academic, but not for the practitioner, is publication in high status scientific journals where sophisticated theory and well-controlled "hard" data are usually the highest priority. On the other hand, a very important incentive for the public service practitioner, but not for the academician, is providing effective service in the context of highly complicated funding and administrative frameworks, involving the need for effective political and communication skills with nonprofessionals, such as lay planning boards, county freeholders, and state legislators. Administration is generally a low priority for academics, something that is to be avoided if possible, and finessed if avoidance is not feasible. In contrast, administration is frequently a high priority for public service practitioners because it is such a crucial element in their agency's financial, clinical, and community success. Academic freedom, a highly cherished value in university settings, emphasizes freedom to follow one's individual intellectual interests in the pursuit of greater truth, no matter what the short-range applied pay-off might be. Yet, in a public agency designed to meet community needs, such individual freedom has to be subjugated to the needs of the community and the agency's funding mandates.

What does all this mean for professional training? From our psychological theory, we know that modelling is a very potent learning process. Are we not then subverting the training of public service practitioners by exposing them to faculty who model academic skills and values that conflict with those of public agency practice? One answer is the "free-standing" professional school. However, as a person who came to Rutgers after four years in the nonacademic world as a program evaluator and administrator in a community mental health center, I am strongly convinced that professional training must have close ties not only to the service-oriented values of the public practice sector, but also to the scientific and intellectual values of the academic sector. Professional training separated from a university setting is susceptible to becoming parochial, doctrinaire, uncritical, and cut-off from an empirically-based approach. On the other hand, of course, primary emphasis upon the university values of research and scholarship has led in the past to academically-oriented "Boulder Model" clinical Ph.D. programs, whose limitations have spawned the professional training movement, as eloquently articulated in the Vail conference report. I believe that it is the creative bringing together of the public practice and academic sectors

FIGURE 5.3

The Integrated Service Center as a Combination of Two Cultures

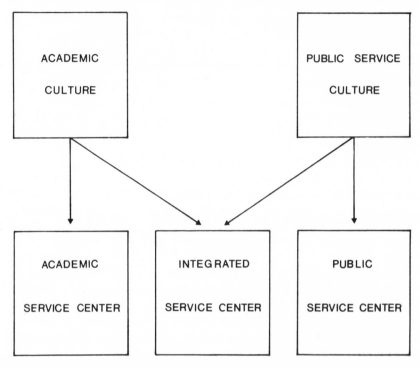

that holds the most potential for professional training programs, both in terms of producing the best public practitioners, and in terms of the program making a unique contribution to the development of more relevant, effective, and accountable human service delivery systems.

How can the academic and the public practitioner cultures be brought together most constructively? The answer lies in a new type of agency, the "integrated service center." Figure 5.3 outlines how such a service center involves joint contributions from the academic and public service cultures, and how such a service center is differentiated from two presently existing types of centers: (a) the "academic service center," such as a teaching hospital or the psychological clinic of a training program, in which community-oriented public service is subordinated to academic training and research; and (b) the "public service center," such as a state mental hospital or community mental health center, that *is* oriented toward community service, but is *not* affiliated with an academic program. The overall mission of the integrated service center is to merge the research and conceptual resources of academia with the operational resources and community service goals of a large, ongoing, high-quality public service agency. Such an agency could create a statewide model of service delivery that is articulated clearly and systematically within human service planning at the local and state levels.

At Rutgers, we have recently stated the case for the Integrated Service Center (ISC) to the deputy director of the New Jersey Division of Mental Health, as follows:

> We at Rutgers view the primary mission of our Professional School as the training of professional psychologists with competencies relevant to and effective within human service agencies, particularly those with a focus upon mental health. Because we believe that a crucial component of good training is exposure to outstanding role models in the actual organizational service setting for which students are being trained, we are strongly committed to becoming closely identified with a model public mental health service program in New Jersey. Moreover, as a publicly supported School of Applied Psychology, we view a major focus of the faculty's research and other scholarly efforts as direct, applied contribution to the development of more relevant, efficient, and effective human service delivery systems.

In discussions with the deputy director and other Division of Mental Health administrators and planners, we came to the conclusion that a community mental health center (CMHC) is a type of organization that is particularly suited to meet the professional school's role-modelling training needs and to provide the best focus for our applied research efforts. Four such centers have been conceptually elaborated and legislatively articulated to be in the forefront of organizational structures for providing comprehensive, community-based, maximally accountable mental health service delivery in integrated coordination with other human services. To date, the Division of Mental Health and the Graduate School of Applied and Professional Psychology administration have arrived at a preliminary consensus that a community mental health center that would be a statewide model in terms of service, training, program demonstration, and applied research would have some of the following characteristics:

a. Provide services that are as relevant as possible to the needs of the CMHC's catchment area;
b. Provide services that are as accountable and cost-effective as possible;
c. Provide services that are formally coordinated with other human service programs in the catchment area;

d. Provide services that are clearly articulated within mental health planning at the catchment area, county, state, and federal levels;

e. Provide an organizational structure that can serve as a statewide test-site for new CMHC service programs and accountability systems;

f. Provide an organizational structure that can facilitate the training of professionals and paraprofessionals throughout the State in model CMHC services; and

g. Integrate the resources of different disciplines, since human services generally, and CMHC services specifically, are multidisciplinary endeavors.

Exactly what is the role of a professional training program in the Integrated Service Center? Clearly, it is not to provide the center with physical facilities or staff for day-to-day functioning. The resources of the professional school are invested into the agency to enrich it and, simultaneously, to provide training in a public service-oriented context. For example, faculty who teach particular intervention techniques, such as multimodal therapy, short-term psychoanalytic therapy, or residential token economies, could hold their classes in the ISC. This would facilitate joint participation of ISC staff, thus breaking down the traditional separation between "teacher" and "service provider," while simultaneously providing continuing education to the ISC staff. In addition, the course instructor could use typical ISC clients and wards for demonstration. This would show immediatley that the demonstrated techniques are applicable to public service settings, and are not unique to specialized teaching clinics and hospitals with clients who are unrepresentative of the catchment area. Also, students who are developing dissertations could be guided to focus on research, evaluation, and program design problems that confront the ISC (i.e., problems for which there is a real, immediate need for systematic investigation). Likewise, the closer the involvement of the faculty in the ISC, the more chance of encouraging faculty to similarly concentrate their research and scholarly efforts upon the real problems that confront a model agency in a statewide service delivery system. It is sometimes forgotten that faculty and student incentives for research and scholarly work create a potentially "free" intellectual resource for attacking the multitude of clinical, organizational, administrative, and planning tasks that confront human service delivery systems.

Thus, when properly designed, an Integrated Service Center should be able to complement the needs and resources of an academic-oriented training program and a public service-oriented community agency. Figure 5.4 summarizes some of the factors involved in this complementarity.

For a detailed illustration of how academic resources can be merged

FIGURE 5.4

**Some Complementary Needs and Resources of Public Service and
Academic Professional Training Programs**

Needs of Public Service Programs

Resources of Academic Training Programs

1. Need for pressing human service problems to be analyzed, and improved solutions to be developed.

1. Theoretical and research person-power.

2. Need for reliable, valid, and feasible program evaluation of services.

2. Methodological expertise.

3. Continuing education needs of service staff.

3. Expertise in training.

4. Need to document clinical, community outreach, administrative, organizational, and systems procedures and their rationale.

4. Ability to conceptualize and document complex issues and procedures in textbooks and other teaching materials.

Needs of Academic Training Programs

Resources of Public Service Programs

5. Need for teaching cases.

5. Available service population.

6. Need to orient students toward public practice.

6. Modeling of high quality, public service roles.

7. Need for relevance: to make research and scholarly work applicable to pressing social problems.

7. Responsiveness to public accountability pressures for relevance of services offered.

8. Need for teaching materials.

8. Complex applied programs which provide numerous case study issues at all levels of service delivery.

---

with the needs of an Integrated Service Center, consider the area of program evaluation. Traditionally, there has been a large separation between the activities of academic researchers, who study psychotherapy outcome, and those of public service practitioners, who deliver psychotherapy services. The assumption has been made that the best techniques and variables for cost-effective therapy would be isolated in the laboratory-like conditions of university-based research; and then these procedures would be incorporated into public service programs.

There are many difficulties with this model. First, the individual studies of academic psychotherapy researchers have usually involved populations that were too small in the context of the degree of statistical differences found to recommend strongly the general adoption of certain therapeutic procedures over others. Also, there have been many special factors embedded in the research settings that prevented their generalization.

Not surprisingly, over the past few years there have been increasing pleas from psychotherapy researchers to conduct large comparison studies with the pooling of data across all cases. But suppose a particular therapeutic program has been shown to be effective in a particular study, how can one be assured that it would be as effective if this program were incorporated into a public-service agency? For example, just because a day hospital sets up a program that is called a "token economy" and has the outward manifestations of a token economy, there is no guarantee that the program will be carried out according to the standards set in the research studies.

In short, there is a need within any particular service agency to continuously monitor the outcomes of its service programs. This is the only way to insure that a particular therapeutic program delivered by a particular staff to a particular group of clients in a particular catchment area at a particular point in time has been effective. Moreover, continual monitoring allows program managers to take action based upon feedback to extend effective programs, and to discontinue or revise ineffective programs. These points are eloquently stated in the 1978 Report of the APA Task Force on Continuing Evaluation in National Health Insurance:

> Programs always change over time. Some of the changes may represent improvements, others may represent degradations. As programs come into being and reach operational stages, staff members may become more skillful, but they may also become biased. Clients may become more faithful, but they may also come to take more for granted. Particularly when programs devised in one setting are copied elsewhere, some of the essential features that made the original program successful may be distorted or lost. It is essential that evaluation be regarded as a continuing process rather than as a discrete, point-in-time event (APA, 1978, p. 311).

Does this mean that psychotherapy outcome research has been useless, and a whole new set of activities called program evaluation should be instituted? Not at all. Rather, the program evaluation of service effectiveness is an applied professional activity whose scientific base has been developed in the academic psychotherapy outcome research literature. All the methodological problems—sample selection, statistical artifacts in change scores, psychometric problems in measuring instruments, etc.—have been articulated and various solutions proposed within this research. This basic science should be applied in designing and performing a program evaluation of therapy services. Therefore, it would seem most appropriate and constructive for an academic training program to come up with program evaluation designs and assessment techniques that can be applied within an Integrated Service Center. The results of these studies could be used in an ongoing way to monitor the services being delivered. Where feasible, experimental or quasi-experimental designs could be instituted to investigate whether present services could be improved and to make comparisons among different staff disciplines. What is crucial here is not simply to have research taking place within the Integrated Service Center, but to have the research resources of the academic training program focused upon developing outcome evaluation that is an integral part of the decision-making structure of the service center.

In sum, practicum training should be an integral part of the total curriculum of a professional education program. While practicum training can be adequately taught within the traditional arrangement of placement in outside agencies and placement in the education program's own psychological clinic, optimal training is best facilitated by the development of Integrated Service Centers. Moreover, it is through such centers that applied psychology as a profession can make a unique contribution to improving human services and human service delivery systems.

References

American Psychological Association. Task Force on Continuing Evaluation in National Health Insurance. Continuing evaluation and accountability controls for a national health insurance program. *American Psychologist,* 1978, *33,* 305-13.

Korman, M. (Ed.) *Levels and patterns of professional training in psychology: Conference proceedings, Vail, Colorado, July 25-30.* Washington, D.C.: American Psychological Association, 1976.

CHAPTER 6

An Innovation in Curriculum Design for Professional Programming

Ronald E. Fox and David A. Rodgers
Wright State University

The development of practitioner-model programs in professional psychology has raised important questions of just how best to articulate such training through the development of innovative curricula. In this chapter, Drs. Fox and Rodgers present the curriculum that was developed at Wright State University. The curriculum was based on a set of guiding principles that required the program to be generic rather than specialty-based, to have its own psychological service delivery system, and to provide for training in program evaluation. The significance of this chapter to the field lies in the unique articulation of the curriculum in relation to the goals of the program and to the principles that directed its development. Further, this chapter provides at least a glimpse of the special value, from the view points of control, flexibility, and resource support, to be gained by a program in professional psychology that is administratively a professional school within a university.

The Wright State University School of Professional Psychology was created by an act of the Ohio General Assembly in the fall of 1976. The enabling legislation called for the establishment of a school within the university that would be authorized to grant the Doctor of Psychology (Psy.D.) degree. The successful passage of this legislation was the culmination of over four years of efforts by a committee of professional psychologists representing the Ohio Psychological Association.

Wright State University is the newest member of Ohio's state-supported university system and has a student body of approximately 13,000. During its first ten years of existence, the university directed its efforts toward establishing a strong undergraduate curriculum and now has begun moving into graduate and professional areas. The Department of Psychology has not previously offered a graduate degree of its own. Consequently, in starting the school, available psychology course offerings were not viewed as appropriate to the needs of doctoral students. A completely new curriculum was required. The curriculum that was developed represents a departure from the typical program in professional psychology.

There were several guiding concepts in the design of the curriculum. It was felt that the program should be generic rather than specialty-based, have its own psychological service delivery system, and provide for training in program evaluation skills. These principles are discussed below.

Our primary guiding concept was that professional psychology training needs are broader than those for clinical psychology. Psychology is one of the few professions that trains for specialty practice in its basic doctoral program. Most other professions focus on broad professional training in the graduate program with specialty training following in postgraduate training. In conceptualizing our curriculum, we felt that psychology should begin to move in this direction. We considered that a school of professional psychology should produce persons who are able to apply the current knowledge and techniques of general psychology in helping clients improve the effectiveness of their behavior. Thus, the curriculum must focus on the role of psychology in general health care, and on improving general behavioral effectiveness, rather than on mental health-related effectiveness only. We believe that students who are generically trained in this fashion and who are knowledgeable about assessment and intervention techniques that apply broadly to many aspects of human behavior will be best prepared for specialization at a later time and we are convinced that a proper knowledge base of relevant psychology subjects enriches the subsequent development of specialty skills.

In concept, design, and time frame, our curriculum was designed to be more analogous to a medical, dental, or law school curriculum than to the curricula that guide the usual clinical psychology Ph.D. programs. For example, the base of medical training is broad knowledge of the anatomy and physiology of normal human functioning. Onto this general base is added specific knowledge of disease processes and symptom syndromes. The medical student is then trained in the professional skills of diagnoses and intervention in a learning-practice-service context that helps him/her obtain the self-concepts and social reflexes that are appropriate to the profession. By analogy, the base of professional training in psychology in the present program is broad knowledge of psychological, sociological, and physiological factors that determine or influence human behavior. Onto this general base is added specific knowledge of psychological aberration, distresses, and strengths, knowledge of malignant as well as supportive environmental influences, and knowledge of patterns of suboptimal as well as optimal coping and interpersonal relationships. The student is trained in the skills of assessment and intervention in a variety of real life professional settings that also direct him/her to the self-conceptions and social reflexes that are appropriate for the professional psychologist.

A second guiding principle in designing our curriculum was the belief that applied training should be accomplished in a school's own psychological delivery system. At Wright State this aim is being accomplished, in part, through a faculty practice plan. All full-time faculty are required to participate in a practice plan that controls monies generated by professional activities in the Psychological Service Center. The monies generated are utilized to supplement faculty salaries and to help support educational programs. All faculty in the school devote about twenty to twenty-five percent of their time to the Psychological Service Center. It is our intent to initiate several programs that will supplement existing clinic and hospital services. For instance, at the present time, there is no local psychometric laboratory available for use by the general public. The faculty will initiate such a laboratory. Students will be utilized as extenders in delivering services and, thus, learn first-hand about the usefulness of psychometricians in psychological practice. The center also has begun to contract for various services with several agencies and clinics. The center pays these agencies for space and the staff time involved in mounting the particular service and, in turn, there is a fee charged for the services provided. In this way it is possible to guarantee that students are not simply assigned to outside agencies for crucial role modeling and socialization into the profession. Instead, students are assigned to the center (an arm of the school) and help provide those services for which the center has contracted.

The third organizing principle in designing the curriculum was that the graduates should be trained in program evaluation. We believe that the practicing professional psychologist is an applied researcher. She/he should approach each client's problems with an empirical attitude and with a professional practice routine that: (a) identifies hypothesis about consequences (including effectiveness) of the intervention procedures, (b) assesses actual outcomes against expected outcomes, and (c) modifies practices in the direction of greater effectiveness. Thus, we designed a curriculum that stresses skills in program control, service by objective, cost-effectiveness assessment, data-based outcome evaluation, and process-relevant record keeping.

Curriculum Goals and Outline

The curriculum goals of the graduate of professional psychology are being accomplished through a dual focus on content knowledge and skills development, and professional development and self-knowledge. The goals of the content knowledge and skills development portions of the curriculum are directed toward providing the student with a broad knowledge of factors that influence human behavior; a detailed knowledge of concepts for understanding, evaluating, and characterizing human behavior; education and training in techniques for professional intervention and appropriate modification of behavior and psychological status; and education and training in procedures of program evaluation, cost-effectiveness, outcome measurement, service-by-objective planning, and other techniques of applied research. Attention to these goals is distributed throughout the four-year curriculum as shown in Table 6.1.

TABLE 6.1

Curriculum Outline

Course Content Area	Year I			Year II				Year III		Year IV	
	F	W	Sp	Su	F	W	Sp	Su	F	W	Sp
Physiology Knowledge Base	X	X	X								
Sociology Knowledge Base	X	X	X								
Psychology Knowledge Base	X	X	X	X	X	X	X				
Knowledge Base, Other Areas	X			X		X	X				
Professional Intervention Techniques	X	X	X	X	X	X		X	X	X	X
Applied Research Methodology				X	X	X	X				
Common Psychological Problem Areas					X	X	X	X	X	X	X
Professional Development and Self-Knowledge	X	X	X	X	X	X	X	X	X	X	X

The third and fourth years are shortened in terms of didactic curriculum because the one-year internship occupies the winter and spring terms of the third year and the summer and fall terms of the fourth year. Professional development and intervention techniques are part of each term's program; physiology, sociology, and psychology are presented each term of the second year. In three of the four quarters of the second year, applied knowledge relevant to professional psychology in fields such as economics and law is covered, as is information in special problem areas. Following the broad knowledge base of the first two years, the third and fourth years are concentrated on professional psychological development, psychological intervention techniques, and further familiarity with common psychological problem areas.

The goals of professional development in psychology emphasize the development of the self as a primary instrument of the professional. This emphasis recognizes that often the applied psychologist utilizes inductive, experientially-based information in addition to "scientific" knowledge. The desired self-development of the students will be directed toward: (a) the acquisition of a thorough knowledge of professional standards, legal statutes, and ethical requirements that guide the profession of psychology; (b) the development of appropriate professional attitudes and personal identity with the psychology profession; (c) the attainment of self-insight, self-knowledge, and insight into prior personal cultural/familial experiences, sufficient to minimize the impact of personal attitudes and biases on professional outcomes and client services; and (d) the attainment of emotional maturity and personal competency such that the resulting graduate will be both an effective person and an effective change agent with a wide range of people.

Professional psychology development and self-knowledge are expected to progress over the four years as follows:

Year	Professional Development and Self-Knowledge Goals
I	Transition into professional training and beginning professional identity.
II	Development of a sense of cultural-societal context of personal attitudes, expectations, values, and perceptions.
III	Integration of personal and professional values and goals into special competency areas.
IV	Continued development of increasing self-awareness, and consolidation and integration of self-identity and professional identity.

The curriculum provides a fifteen-quarter (including internship), eleven-month-per-year program, divided into four quarters of eleven weeks each, parallel to the Wright State University academic calendar. The arrangement within each quarter includes a nine week teaching block (eight weeks of content and one week for exams) and a two week "selective" period. The first year consists of fall, winter, and spring quarters. The remaining years include a summer quarter as well. Except in the field-work or practicum apprenticeship year which follows a different calendar, this schedule provides for approximately two months of combined holiday and vacation time during the year.

The curriculum provides for individualized and elective learning during the selectives. The term arrangements are shown in Figure 6.1. Most quarters are followed by a two week selective period. Each selective is an intensive, in-depth experience in a particular subject offered by one or more faculty experts. These are designed to enrich and extend the student's core curriculum content. A selective will not be limited to a fixed number of hours and provides for an immersion in a subject. Selectives are planned to utilize outside consultants and team teaching approaches. The selectives will be individualized to the particular needs and interests of particular groups of students.

Class units represent one hour of class and approximately two hours of preparation. Each term consists of nineteen units of combined class and laboratory. Since each term is eight teaching weeks long instead of the usual ten weeks, the nineteen units amount to approximately fifteen conventional units per term. However, the selectives add to the unit load of the students. All students are expected to take the full program. Progression is on the basis of overall competency, not on the basis of accumulated credit hours.

The amount of lecture-didactic presentation in class is kept to a minimum and active student-teacher interaction is emphasized. Class interaction is designed to foster active learning rather than passive absorption. Objective content is conveyed largely through written material and reading assignments, to be completed as class preparation.

This fifteen quarter, full-time, eleven-month-per-year program was designed with several considerations in mind. Practicum agencies are programmed for provision of services throughout the entire calendar year. Student training needs to be integrated into these services in a meaningful way, so that students can learn by meeting the needs of constituent clients and so that agencies can depend on the students to render professionally meaningful services. Therefore, the practicum services provided by students of the school parallel the ongoing nature of the client services. Socialization of the students into the appropriate attitudes, roles, self-perceptions, and social responsibilities of the professional psychologist is an important goal of the program. The professional responsibilities toward meeting client needs do not correspond to an academic calendar. As a consequence, the service delivery function of the school and of the faculty continue year round. Finally, the amount of material to be assimilated for competency as a professional psychologist is enormous, exceeding what can be encompassed in a nine-month pro-

FIGURE 6.1

Schematic Outline of the Psy.D. Curriculum

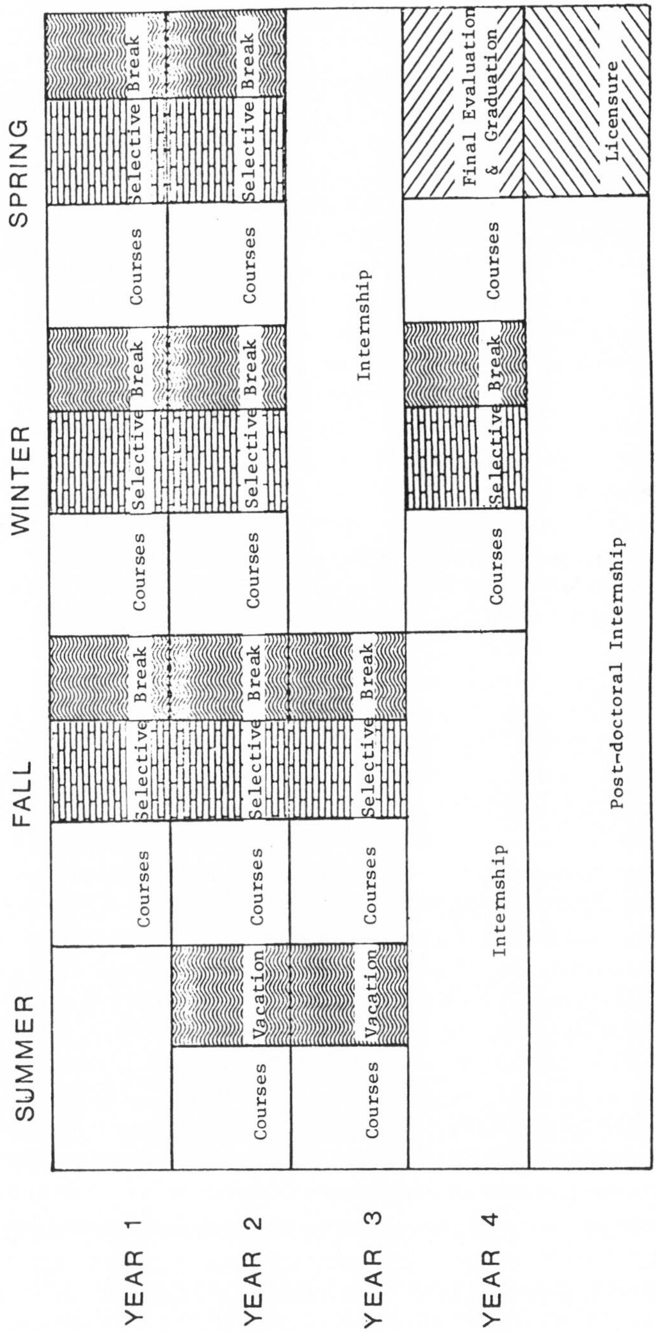

gram. The eleven-month format allows coverage of more of this critical material.

The eight-one-two (eight weeks core instruction, one week exams, two weeks individualized instruction) program has several advantages within the present curriculum. During the shortened term, students are not distracted by other elective courses or academic interests. Subsequently, during the selective period, several kinds of worthwhile individualized instructional programs can be incorporated. These selective periods offer four specific advantages: intervention or assessment techniques can be taught better in time-intensive workshops than in the spaced-learning conventional class format, individualized instruction for subgroups of students with special needs can be achieved, immediate review of troublesome material from the previous terms can be accomplished and the selectives also allow some individualized specialization. In summary, the "eight-one-two" term arrangement combines many advantages of an intensive lockstep core program with considerable concurrent opportunity for individualized learning experiences.

An outline of the curriculum is presented in Table 6.2 with approximate faculty contact hours shown for each course in each term.

Curriculum Content

All purposive behavior involves the performance of a physiologic organism, subject to environmental constraints and influences in a social context, regulated by the information processing characteristics of the subject, including stored knowledge and stored distortions of knowledge, perceptual capacity, motivations, behavior patterns, and other psychological characteristics. The understanding of human behavior therefore requires a knowledge of the physiological, sociological, and psychological dimensions that characterize it. For this reason the first level of skills training concerns relevant knowledge of these various dimensions. The other dimensions of the curriculum follow from this base: philosophy, law, economics, applied research methodology, program control, special problem areas, skill in the various professional intervention techniques with emphasis on both assessment and behavior change techniques, self-knowledge, and professional development content areas.

Physiology Knowledge Base

The curriculum covers neurology, endocrinology, and other parameters of physiology that have special relevance for purposive behavior.

Among the other dimensions, cardiovascular reserve, nutritional status, the impact of drugs, genetics, and behavior genetics also are covered.

Sociology Knowledge Base

Information is provided on as many facets of contemporary culture as possible, with special emphasis on those aspects that are known to be associated with psychological problems. These foci for psychological problems include the family, the work environment, minorities, urban settings, rural settings, the criminal justice system, and government and social institutions. Perspectives from law, business administration, anthropology, sociology, political science, and economics also are included. Information in these areas is presented in forms relevant to the understanding of the problems of the potential psychology client. For example, knowledge about prejudice emphasizes the emotional impact of being the object of prejudice, and its impact on reducing the options of both the psychologist and the client.

Special efforts are made to avoid transmitting knowledge in a form that carries forward the perpetuation of problems. This aspect of the curriculum cannot be communicated or ensured by course titles alone, but is essential and is being assessed continually through curriculum evaluation.

Psychology Knowledge Base

Advanced knowledge in several areas of psychology essential to the practitioner is covered. These areas include learning, perception, motivation, cognition, personality, developmental, and ideopathic and nomothetic concepts. These areas are traditional in all doctoral psychology programs and will not be elaborated here. However, the focus of these courses is on the needs of the professional practitioner, not on those of the research scholar.

Knowledge Base, Other Areas

In addition to knowledge in the biopsychosocial areas, information from other areas also is of importance to the practicing psychologist. General systems theory and epistemology help to place the work of the professional in perspective. The political system and the legislative process have profound implications for behavior, both by structuring the context in which behavior occurs and by offering a vehicle of change that

TABLE 6.2
Program Outline

YEAR I

Summer	Hours	Fall	Hours	Winter	Hours	Spring	Hours
		Professional Development	1	Professional Development	1	Professional Development	1
		General Body Systems & Endocrinology	2	Neurology & Neuropathology	2	Proseminar in Pharmacology & Nutrition	2
		Proseminar in Sociology: Urban & Rural Settings	3	Proseminar in Sociology: Minorities	2	Proseminar in Sociology: The Family & Other Systems	2
		Advanced Human Development: Infancy Through Adolescence	2	Advanced Human Development: Adulthood & Gerontology	2	Advanced Social Psychology	2
		Intelligence & Aptitude Testing	2	Psychodiagnostic Assessment & Interviewing	4	Neuropsychological Assessment	2
		Theory of Knowledge	3	Advanced Personality Theory	2	Advanced Personality Theory	4
		Related Practicum/Labs	6	Related Practicum/Labs	6	Related Practicum/Labs	6
			19		19		19

YEAR II

Summer	Hours	Fall	Hours	Winter	Hours	Spring	Hours
Professional Development	1	Professional Development	1	Professional Development	1	Professional Development	1
Proseminar in Psychology: Mechanisms of Perception & Motivation	2	Behavior Genetics	2	Special Seminar: Org. & Management Processes	3	Concepts of Psychopathology	3
Personality Testing	3	Intervention Techniques	2	Proseminar in Psychology: Behavior Modification	2	Individual Psychotherapy	3
Proseminar in Political Science	2	Proseminar in Psychology: Mechanisms of Learning & Memory	3	Proseminar in Prejudice, Discrimination, & Stereotyping	2	Gerontology	2
Applied Research	3	Applied Research	2	Applied Research	3	Applied Research	2
Related Practicum/Labs	8	Human Factor Engineering	3	Proseminar in Law	2	Special Seminar: Influence of Economic Systems on Behavior	3
		Related Practicum/Labs	7	Related Practicum/Labs	6	Related Practicum/Labs	5
	19		19		19		19

YEAR III

Summer	Hours	Fall	Hours	Winter	Hours	Spring	Hours
Professional Development	1	Professional Development	1	Full Time Internship	1	Full Time Internship	
Proseminar in Criminology & Delinquency	2	Alcohol & Substance Abuse	2	a) Immersion in professional service delivery under supervision of school faculty.			
Family Processes	2	Treatment of Marital & Sexual Problems	3	b) Experience in several areas of practice, i.e., clinical, community, industrial.			
Assessment via Simulation Techniques	3	Industrial Consultation	2				
Group Psychotherapy	2	Special Seminar: Conflict Management	1				
Intervention Techniques	1	Stereotype Modification	2				
Related Practicum/Labs	8	Related Practicum/Labs	7				
	19		18				

YEAR IV

Summer	Hours	Fall	Hours	Winter	Hours	Spring	Hours
Full Time Internship Continued		Full Time Internship Continued		Professional Development	1	Professional Development	1
a) Significant focus on student's primary area of interest in practice.				Forensic Psychology	2	Development Crises: Management & Treatment	2
b) Experience in applied dimension of professional specialization.				Proseminar in Sociology: Use of Social Institutions	2	Crisis Intervention	1
				Treatment Approaches with the Handicapped	3	Professional Practice Seminar	1
				Habit & Life Style Modification Approaches	3	Professional Applications of the Learning Process	2
				Related Practicum/Labs	8	Related Practicum/Labs	7
					19		14

can be used both by professionals and clients as a means of effective coping. Knowledge of the law as it applies to the average citizen (concerning family rights and obligations for example) and of the court systems with which clients might become involved is needed by the practicing psychologist, both to understand the problems that clients might encounter and to counsel clients about legal directions they might explore to deal with psychological problems. Similarly, economic systems profoundly shape behavior and determine patterns of effective and ineffective coping. They, therefore, are structures about which the professional psychologist should have sophisticated knowledge.

Professional Intervention Techniques

Concepts that have proved useful for evaluating, classifying, and characterizing behaviors, psychological functioning, cognitive functioning, sociologic functioning, and physiologic functioning have been added to the foundation of knowledge about factors affecting human behaviors. Course work includes techniques of neuropsychological assessment of central nervous system structural and functional integrity; psychological assessment of psychosomatic, emotional, and cognitive status; assessment of interpersonal habits and skills; and assessment of group interaction patterns. Curriculum emphasis is on understanding both the potentials and the limitations of standard psychological assessment devices, as well as on mastery of competency in using the devices. Emphasis also is placed on creative adaptation of observational approaches and other assessment procedures to the unique demands of the client.

Applied Research Methodology

The skills of program evaluation and cost-effectiveness assessment, establishing service-by-objective records that clarify effective strategies in accomplishing treatment goals, and the application of research in order to evaluate new professional techniques complete the primary areas of training in the curriculum. By incorporating proper strategies for evaluating service effectiveness into the basic system of delivering services, the professional can force attention to his/her own professional competencies and treatment strategies.

Common Psychological Problem Areas

There are many recurring areas of human interaction from which persons often develop psychological problems. These areas include, for example, the problems of prejudice, aging, parenting, marriage, sex, substance abuse, and the handicapped. Attention to these problem areas constitutes much of the work of the practicing psychologist. Therefore, these areas are given substantial emphasis in the curriculum, particularly toward the end of the program so that the student can build upon earlier knowledge and skills.

Professional Development and Self-Knowledge

Many intervention procedures involve intimate interactions between the psychologist and the client. To be effective, the professional psychologist must have sufficient self-knowledge, self-awareness, and self-insight to avoid improper impositions of his/her own arbitrary personal value system and be able to appropriately use his or her own personality in interpersonal interaction to benefit the client. Indeed, the primary tools of the professional psychologist are his/her own personality characteristics, beliefs, and value systems. Thorough knowledge and skillful use of self are essential to effective practice. Self-development of the students of the school is therefore a fundamental aspect of the curriculum.

Students are familiarized with the legal and quasi-legal professional codes that have developed in psychology to guide the professional and to protect the client from some of the potential errors of professional practice. Among these codes are the Ohio Licensing Law, the American Psychological Association (APA) Code of Ethics, and the APA Standards for Providers of Psychological Services, as well as a variety of associated legal statutes and professional guidelines. The application of these codes to model problems transforms them from theoretical to practical documents.

Students also are made familiar with the history and sociology of professions in general, psychology being presented in relation to other professions. There is constant reiteration, in all of the courses, of the theme that the primary reason for the course work is to prepare the student to assume the responsibilities of the professional psychologist.

Knowledge of professional ethics and practices in psychology is not in itself enough to insure adequate service to, or protection of, the client. Those codified ethics and practices must be translated into personal attitudes and commitments that are far more powerful and far more dependable determiners of professional behavior. The development of appropriate professional attitudes therefore is critical. Appropriate attitudes are modeled by the faculty and, when possible, specifically identified and characterized. Similarly, student attitudes are noted and evaluated on a par with academic performance. All students are treated

TABLE 6.3
Core Curriculum

YEAR I

Summer	Fall	Winter	Spring
	Professional Development: The Profession of Psychology—Statutory and regulatory bases, goals and definitions of the profession. Beginning exploration of personal goals to be achieved via the profession. (One Class Unit, One Lab Unit)*	*Professional Development: History of the Profession*—Modes of practice. Beginning assessment of personal sensitivities to different cultural and emotional perspectives, needs and strengths. (One Class Unit, One Lab Unit)	*Professional Development: Systems of Program Evaluation and Control*—How to design self-corrective procedures into professional practice. Beginning experience in assessing impact of one's own interventions on others and in establishing a goal and assessing progress toward it. (One Class Unit, One Lab Unit)
	Intelligence and other aptitude testing—Theories of intelligence and aptitude—primary mental abilities and general factors concepts. Administration and interpretation of the standard tests of intelligence (including the Stanford-Binet, WAIS, and WISC-R) and of aptitude. (Two Class Units, One Lab Unit)	*Psychodiagnostic and assessment Interviewing*—The Professional assessment interview, structured, open ended, historically focused, problem focused, feeling-tone focused. (Two Class Units, Two Lab Units)	*Neuropsychological assessment procedures*—The use of psychological procedures to assess presence or absence of central nervous system organic dysfunction. Proficiency will be developed in the use of various memory scales, aphasia tests, and standard neuropsychological batteries. (Two Class Units, Two Lab Units)
	Advanced Human Development—Infancy through adolescence—Primary focus will be on how normal developmental processes and their variants can produce psychological problems and can be used to understand and help overcome psychological problems. (Two Class Units, One Lab Unit)	*Advanced Human Development—Adulthood and gerontology*—Primary focus will be on normal development and decline, their relationships to causing, or contributing to solutions of psychological problems, and their usefulness in understanding psychological problems. (Two Class Units, One Lab Unit)	*Advanced personality theory—behavioral, expectational, cognitive*—Continued exploration of the relationships of personality theories to professional practice, with attention to the implications that the different theories have for var-
		Advanced personality theory—dynamic theories and self theories—Relationships of personality theo-	

General body systems and endocrinology—Review of musculoskeletal, cardiovascular, gastrointestinal, and hematological systems as these relate to behavior, psychological states, and psychological problems. Interaction of endocrine function and psychological state. Consideration of the endocrine system as a "slow signal" information processing system. (Two Class Units, One Lab Unit)

Proseminar in sociology: urban and rural settings—Examination of characteristics of urban settings and of rural settings that can contribute to psychological problems, their understanding, and their solutions. Exploration of sociologic variables that facilitate and that inhibit effective communication between psychologist and client. (Three Class Units, Two Lab Units)

Theory of Knowledge—General system theory, epistemology, philosophy of knowledge, of science, of professionalism. Consideration of the general philosophical and epistemologic structure in which

ries to professional practice, implications for professional practice of alternative view points; several dynamic and self theories will be covered and contrasted with each other. (Four Class Units)

Neurology and neuropathology—The primary neurological mechanisms and pathways involved in behavior. Neuropathology as it relates to psychological practice. (Two Class Units, One Lab Unit)

Proseminar in sociology: minorities—Examination of the social structures of minority status as they contribute to particular reinforced patterns of behavior, to psychological problems, and to potential for resolution of problems. (Two Class Units, One Lab Unit)

ious intervention strategies. Behavioral, expectational and cognitively mediated theories will be the focus of attention. (Four Class Units)

Advanced social psychology—small group process and social role theory. Attention to the impact of group process on behavior change. Group process theories underlying the practice of group psychotherapy. (Two Class Units, One Lab Unit)

Proseminar in pharmacology and nutrition—The major neuroleptics, tranquilizers, antidepressants, mood elevators, and sedatives; their behavioral indicators, side effects, and contraindications. Nutrition as it affects mood, vital capacity, and behavior. The pharmacology of pleasure drugs. (Two Class Units, One Lab Unit)

Proseminar in sociology: the family and other systems—The sociologic structure of the family and other interaction systems, including the industrial systems, in which psychological problems occur. Attention will be given to the ways in which these systems reinforce the

TABLE 6.3 (Continued)

YEAR I

Summer	Fall	Winter	Spring
	the psychologist-client relationship takes place, with attention to the most appropriate perspectives for the practicing psychologist.' (Three Class Units)		psychological problems and inhibit their solutions as well as to the ways in which they can be used to facilitate solutions and prevent regressions. (Two Class Units, One Lab Unit)
	TOTAL UNITS: 19 (13 Class Units + 6 Lab Units)	TOTAL UNITS: 19 (13 Class Units + 6 Lab Units)	TOTAL UNITS: 19 (13 Class Units + 6 Lab Units)

YEAR II

Summer	Fall	Winter	Spring
Professional Development: Exploration of group process, as a participant observer—Task focus of the group is to review and evaluate the first year of the program. (One Class Unit, One Lab Unit) *Personality testing*—objective and projective personality testing. Use of tests for diagnosis, for assessment of strengths and weaknesses. Normative standardization and minority concerns. Beginning developments of professional proficiency in the use of tests. (Three Class Units, Two Lab Units)	*Professional Development: Participant observation and role-playing*—Practice with various intervention techniques—students using each other as subjects, under close faculty supervision—with behavior modification, biofeedback, hypnosis, and other intervention techniques. The focus will be simultaneously on developing skill in the use of techniques, learning about the techniques and the client's likely reactions to them, and learning about self. (One Class Unit, One Lab Unit)	*Professional Development: Dealing with conflict*—Participation under close faculty supervision in consciousness-raising, confrontation, and other conflict resolution procedures. The focus would be simultaneously on developing skill, learning about the techniques, and learning about self. (One Class Unit, One Lab Unit) *Proseminar in psychology: behavior modification*—Contingency reward systems, practical utilization of behavior modification techniques in applied settings, ethical	*Professional Development: Professional and personal issues*—The ethics and standards of practice of the profession, related professional guidelines, continuing exploration of personal sensitivity to body language, subtle verbal cues, cultural sensitivities, and other indirect systems of communication. Primary use will be made of videotapes and laboratory materials. (One Class Unit, One Lab Unit) *Individual psychotherapy*—(Note that a number of other courses and practica also deal with this

Proseminar in psychology—mechanisms of perception and of motivation—Examination of the role of perception in such clinical phenomena as conversion reaction syndromes, hallucinations, pain syndromes, phobias, delusions. Theories of motivation. Motivational considerations in concepts of psychopathology and psychological intervention strategies. (Two Class Units, Two Lab Units)

Applied research—Statistics, research design, concepts of inference, use of calculators and computers. (Three Class Units, One Lab Unit)

Proseminar in Political Science—The legislative process as a vehicle of behavior regulation and of behavior change. (Two Class Units, Two Lab Units)

and legal considerations. Client-controlled behavior modification techniques. (Two Class Units, Two Lab Units)

Intervention Techniques—biofeedback, hypnosis, role playing, assertiveness training. (Two Class Units, Two Lab Units)

Human factors engineering problems—Including man-machine interface systems, product liability problems, psychological dimensions of prosthesis utilization. (Two Class Units, One Lab Unit)

Proseminar in psychology-mechanisms of learning and of memory—Focus on translation of learning theory and theories of memory into practical application, in the classroom, in the industrial setting, at home, in continuing education programs. The interaction of emotional state with memory and learning. Methods of compensation for cognitive and physical deficits that may interfere with normal process of learning or of memory. (Two Class Units, Two Lab Units)

Proseminar in prejudice, discrimination and stereotyping—Psychological problems of minorities and the roles of social stereotyping in contributing to both the problems and their solutions. Attention to the extent to which different intervention strategies may reflect and stabilize rather than alleviate inappropriate stereotyping. (Two Class Units, One Lab Unit)

Behavior genetics—What is known about the genetic dimension as it impacts on various psychological capacities, problems, and behavior patterns. Methods of genetic analysis. Nature-nurture controversies and workable perspectives for the practicing psychologist. (Two Class Units)

Special Seminar: Organization and management processes—The understanding of organizational and management processes from the perspective of the professional psychologist working with top management and the personalities of managers. Attention to conflicts between management effectiveness and personal satisfaction of managers. Examination of management styles and appropriate versus inappropriate organizational structures. (Three Class Units)

Applied research—Program evaluation, cost effectiveness, accountability controls. (Three Class Units, One Lab Unit)

topic, under other titles.) Coverage of basic theoretical approaches and practical applications. (Three Class Units, Two Lab Units)

Gerontology—The problems and opportunities of aging. Geriatric institutions. Psychological intervention strategies for common problems of the elderly, boredom, loneliness, decline in physical vigor, sexual frustration, wisdom without influence, etc. (Two Class Units)

Concepts of psychopathology—History of treatment approaches for the emotionally disturbed. DSM II and III. CHAMPUS Behavioral Classification Criterion Sets. Medical models, psychological models, cultural norm models.

Applied research—Evaluating research literature, writing research reports, implementing program evaluation or procedure assessment. (Two Class Units, Two Lab Units)

Special seminar: Influence of economic systems on behavior—Examination of the role that economic systems have on contributing to, stabilizing, or helping to alleviate psychological problems. The economics of disability and of

TABLE 6.3 (Continued)

YEAR II

Summer	Fall	Winter	Spring
Professional Development: Group Processes and Personal Development—Continuing exploration of group process, as a participant observer. The task focus of the group will be to review and evaluate the second year of the program. During this period, each student will also be expected to plan a personal professional development course or experience for the fall term and to be continued through the internship year, and to secure approval of	Applied research—Advanced statistics, use of computers and computer services, correlational and multivariate procedures, development and maintenance of data bases. (Three Class Units, One Lab Unit)	Proseminar in law—Those dimensions of law that are commonly encountered by psychologists such as divorce law, legal rights, and obligations of children and of parents, small claims courts and how to use them, juvenile courts, domestic courts, legal aid societies, the appropriate use of attorneys. (Two Class Units)	different third-party-payment arrangements for treatment. Economic systems as incentive systems. (Three Class Units)

YEAR III

Summer	Fall	Winter	Spring
	Professional Development: Personal Development—Beginning implementation of, and further refinement of, the personal professional development plan, developed in the previous term. (Two Lab Units) Industrial Consultation—The conceptual bases of industrial consultation, the similarities and differences to other types of consultation; practical implications of concepts. (Two Class Units, One Lab Unit)	Internship (a) Immersion in professional service delivery under supervision of school faculty. (b) Experience in several areas of practice, i.e., clinical, community, industrial.	Internship

committee that will also have responsibility for assisting students in the development of appropriate plans. (One Class Unit, One Lab Unit)

Group Psychotherapy—Coverage of major theoretical approaches to group treatment; practical applications. (Two Class Units, One Lab Unit)

Participation Observation—Family games, hypothetical problems, bibliotherapy. (Three Class Units, One Lab Unit)

Intervention Techniques—Directed fantasy, dream interpretation, and related techniques. (One Class Unit, One Lab Unit)

Family Processes—Parenting problems, and problems of children, with attention to different norms. (Two Class Units, Two Lab Units)

Proseminar in criminology and delinquency—Psychological conceptions of criminality and of delinquency—personality dimensions, constitutional or physiological dimensions, sociological dimensions. Modes of psychological intervention, with attention to evidence concerning effectiveness and ineffectiveness. (Two Class Units, Two Lab Units)

sciousness raising, and related approaches. Focus will be on the identification of common stereotypes in differing groups and individuals; methods of demonstrating their existence to clients, and procedures for modification. (Two Class Units, One Lab Unit)

Special Seminar: Management of conflict and conflict negotiation—The role of the psychologist in stress management; the use and management of conflict in industrial/business settings, in organizations, and between individuals. (Two Class Units, One Lab Unit)

Alcohol and other substance abuse—Coverage of the causes, prevention and major treatment methods of alcoholism, drug addiction, and general substance abuse. Attention will also be given to the so-called "social drugs," the major research findings about them and their effects on behavior. (Two Class Units, One Lab Unit)

Treatment of marital, sexual, dating, and other interpersonal problems—The understanding and management of intimate, interpersonal difficulties from an interactional point of view. (Three Class Units, Two Lab Units)

TABLE 6.3 (Continued)

YEAR IV

Summer	Fall	Winter	Spring
Internship (a) Significant focus of student's primary area of interest in practice. (b) Experience in applied dimensions of professional specialization.	Internship	*Professional Development: Synthesis*—Group debriefing and sharing of professional experiences and insights during the internships. Beginning individual differentiation into specialty focus, and group discussion of options, pros and cons, etc., of the various future professional goals. Discussion of current legal issues, legislative and regulatory processes, professional organizations. (One Class Unit, Two Lab Units) *Habit and Life Style Modification Approaches*—Smoking, obesity, drug abuse, lack of exercise, etc., will be studied as purposive behavior which impact on general health, which relate to personality style, and which are subject to psychological influence. (Three Class Units, Two Lab Units) *Forensic Psychology*—Trial testi-	*Professional Development: Summary*—Practical matters of professional practice, such as malpractice insurance, accounting procedures, billing procedures, supervisory practice. Update on postdoctoral internship options. Critique of the overall training experience, with feedback advice to the School concerning perceived strengths and weaknesses and recommended change. (Three Class Units, One Lab Unit) *Professional Applications of the Learning Process*—In Industry, in schools, in continuing education. (Two Class Units, One Lab Unit) *Crisis Intervention*—The function and utilization of crisis-oriented treatment strategies in emergency services, suicide prevention, "hotline" services, etc. (One Class Unit, Two Lab Units)

mony, expert witness, involuntary commitment, competency hearing, custody hearing, disability hearing, etc. (Two Class Units, One Lab Unit)

Treatment approaches with the handicapped—Including mentally retarded, institutionalized, other special groups. (Three Class Units, Two Lab Units)

Proseminar in Sociology: Use of Social Institutions—Familiarization with social support institutions such as BVR, AA, Family Service, Welfare Department, Legal Aid, etc., and how the practitioner can work with them for benefit of clients. (One Class Unit, One Lab Unit)

Developmental Crises: Management and treatment—Focus will be on the identification and management of "normal developmental crises" in otherwise well-functioning persons. (Two Class Units, One Lab Unit)

Professional Practice Seminar—Final wrapup. (One Class Unit, Two Lab Units) as professionals and are expected to behave as such. Immediately follow-ing entrance into the program, they are required to have professional psychological interaction with clients, where, under supervision they are required to bear the burden of professional responsibility for their im-pact on real people.

Ethical commitments and professional attitudes do not replace true self-knowledge. A designated amount of specific course work is directed toward development of self-knowledge, such as participant-observation studies of group process in which the observers also are the members of the group they observe. Courses directed toward heightening the sen-sitivity of intrapersonal and interpersonal observation, understanding the multiple perspectives from which a situation can be judged, and identification of prejudice also are offered. In addition, since most of the curriculum concerns techniques and perspectives for understanding hu-man behavior, students are expected to use those procedures to become informed about their own behavior and its roots as a means to better understand the techniques and as a way of developing increasing insight into their own psychological characteristics.

Summary of Course Content

In Table 6.3, a detailed outline of the core curriculum is presented. This table is intended to communicate the uniqueness of the curriculum and the integrated configurations that distinguish the program of the School of Professional Psychology at Wright State University.

Curriculum Evaluation

Because each course is tailored to the specific goals of the school, course titles alone do not insure an appropriate educational experience for the students. All courses are taught at an advanced postbaccalaureate level and follow customary procedures for insuring quality control. For each course, detailed content is outlined, specific goals stated, and "prod-uct outcome" criteria are developed in order to allow for teaching-by-objective. These content, goal, and criteria guidelines enable each course to be monitored and evaluated continuously by the Curriculum Evalua-tion Committee (CEC).

The purpose of the CEC is to facilitate the development of learning experiences that meet the goals and objectives of the school. The follow-ing duties are the responsibility of this committee: (a) to provide input into curriculum development to insure that the goals and objectives of the courses are framed in a manner to facilitate evaluation, (b) to evaluate the process and outcomes of the existing curriculum, and to report results and recommendations to the faculty, (c) to provide leadership in the ongoing development and improvement of the curriculum, (d) to review all proposals for additions or changes in the curriculum for the purpose of developing methods of evaluation and to determine whether the proposal is consistent with the overall goals of the program, and (e) to obtain and use regular feedback from students and faculty about each part of the curriculum. Reports designed to identify deficiencies and strengths are issued by the CEC on the courses as a whole, as well as on the modules within each course. These reports range from recommendations for possible changes and deletions in existing courses, to recommendations for additions to the curriculum to meet the overall goals of the program.

Summary

The curriculum presented here has many features that distinguish it from curricula offered in Ph.D. psychology programs and, to a lesser degree, the curricula offered in other schools of professional psychology. Particularly notable differences include breadth of the curriculum content, the use of "lockstep" courses to assure a common professional knowledge base, the achievement of flexibility and specialization through integrated "selectives," the maintenance of control of the one-year internship in order to coordinate it within the curriculum, and the utilization of the curriculum to achieve self-knowledge as well as to develop a skilled professional psychologist. The curriculum is demanding, intense, and idealistic. It is presented here for the purpose of sharing our thoughts with like-minded colleagues. Like any other group that has ever struggled with designing a curriculum, we believe that our proposal is a contributiuon to the field that can serve as a model for others.

CHAPTER 7

The Accreditation Process: Facing New Challenges [1]

Meredith P. Crawford
American Psychological Association

Just as there have been many developments within professional psychology pro-
gramming over the past several years, so too there have been major changes in the
process by which the American Psychological Association (APA) conducts pro-
grammatic accreditation. The criteria used by APA in evaluating psychology train-
ing programs also have been revised recently and many of the developments within
the accreditation process as well as in the accreditation criteria have special signifi-
cance for practitioner-model educational programs. Although Dr. Crawford did not
attend the Virginia Beach conference, he nevertheless was invited to contribute this
chapter because the recent developments within APA accreditation are so important
to professional psychology. In this chapter, Dr. Crawford begins by tracing some of
the major trends in the development of APA accreditation and notes also the recent
rapid growth in the number of programs seeking accreditation. Thereafter, he notes
some of the recent procedural changes associated with the new accreditation process
and discusses in general terms the new accreditation criteria, which, he comments,
reflect an increasing recognition and acceptance of the practitioner educational
model, but are designed to apply to both practitioner and scientist-professional
model programs. Finally, the chapter closes with some general comments about the
challenges to be faced in the next few years by the APA accreditation process as it
attempts to keep abreast with the changes within educational programs in psy-
chology.

Challenges Met: Brief History

During and immediately after World War II, the usefulness of psychology in many applied fields became abundantly apparent, not only in
the solution of practical problems through research and development,
but also in the emergence of professional practice by psychologists in
health-related and other fields. Quality of the products of research and

development is assured by objective procedures of test and evaluation. Quality of professional practice is assured by examination of the codes and practices of the profession and by the nature of the education and training of its practitioners. It is with the assessment of the latter that the process of accreditation is concerned. The results of such assessments are useful to the program being evaluated because of the efforts made by the program to meet the requirements of the accrediting agency. They are also used by prospective students in choosing where to study, by state licensing and credentialing bodies as indices of adequacy of the professional preparation of candidates, by fund-granting agencies as a guide to quality programs, and by the general public as assurance that a program may be expected to turn out competent professionals.

The original challenge to the APA for assessment and accreditation of clinical psychology came in the late 1940s from federal agencies (the Veterans Administration, the Public Health Service, and the Army Surgeon General) that wished to know which programs could be expected to produce competent professionals and would be worthy of financial support. The APA first undertook the accreditation of doctoral programs in clinical psychology in 1948, in counseling psychology in 1950, and in school psychology in the late 1960s. The first set of criteria was developed in 1947 (Report to the Committee on Training in Clinical Psychology, 1947) and has been revised from time to time thereafter. An early codification of the criteria was published by the Education and Training Board (1958). A summary account of the early history of APA accreditation was prepared by Goodstein and Ross (1966). In 1973, the APA published *Accreditation Procedures and Criteria,* which was in use through August 31, 1980, after which the criteria adopted by the Council of Representatives in January 1979, and slightly amended in January 1980, became mandatory for all accredited doctoral and predoctoral internship programs (APA, 1980).

Successive changes in the criteria have reflected many of the findings and recommendations of the several national conferences on professional training in psychology. The original one, held in Boulder in 1947 (Raimy, 1950), established the "scientist-professional" model. Succeeding conferences included ones at Stanford University in 1955 (Strother, 1956), Miami Beach in 1958 (Roe, Gustad, Moore, Ross, & Skodak, 1959), Chicago in 1965 (Hoch, Ross, & Winder, 1966), and in Vail in 1973 (Korman, 1976).

Accreditation of predoctoral internship programs by the APA began in 1956, based on criteria developed during the early 1950s, as recorded in reports by the APA Committee on Training in Clinical Psychology (1950), the Committee on Counselor Training (1952), and in accordance with criteria first published in 1958 (Education and Training Board, 1958).

As of June 1980, a total of 160 doctoral and 202 predoctoral internship programs were included in the list of APA-accredited programs at full, provisional, or probationary status. The doctoral list was comprised of 117 clinical, 26 counseling, 14 school, and 3 combined scientific-professional programs. Since the fall of 1978, there has been a sharp rise in the rate of applications for accreditation. For example, between October 1978 and June 1980, 20 doctoral and 64 internship programs were added to the list. A review of the actions of the Committee on Accreditation since 1971 reveals that about 80 percent of doctoral and 82 percent of internship programs were awarded full or provisional accreditation on initial applications.

National Recognition of Accrediting Agencies

The legitimacy of the activities of organizations that accredit educational and training programs in the United States is recognized by two agencies: a nongovernmental body, the Council on Postsecondary Accreditation (COPA) and the secretary of education of the United States acting through the Division of Eligibility and Agency Evaluation (DEAE). There are two kinds of accrediting agencies: those which accredit entire institutions and those which accredit programs of study. The 52 accrediting agencies recognized by COPA are organized in terms of this distinction into the Assembly of Institutional Accrediting Bodies and the Assembly of Specialized Accrediting Bodies. APA holds membership in the latter.

To gain recognition by COPA or by the U.S. Department of Education an accrediting agency must file and orally defend a petition that demonstrates that the agency operates in such a way as to meet the detailed sets of criteria of each recognition body. During 1979, the APA was successful in gaining continued recognition by both of these bodies for the accreditation of doctoral programs in professional psychology (clinical, counseling, school, and combined professional-scientific psychology) and by DEAE for predoctoral internships (COPA does not recognize the accreditation of internship programs). This means that the APA program is in compliance with the criteria of both agencies—criteria that concern the public responsibility and procedural nature of the accreditation process rather than the scientific-professional-technical nature of the substantive criteria currently in use. COPA recently published *A Guide to Recognized Accrediting Agencies* (Peterson, 1980) and a listing of *Accredited Institutions of Postsecondary Education* (Harris, ed., 1979).

Similar listings have been published by the former U.S. Office of Education (Ross, et al., 1979).

The Process and Procedures of APA Accreditation

Beginning during the latter part of 1978, a substantial refinement has taken place in the process of accreditation as performed by the APA. While its objectives and general mode of operation have remained the same, the adoption of new criteria for both doctoral and internship programs in early 1979 became a stimulus for amplification and updating of procedures and the several documents that implement the program. An accreditation handbook was published by the APA in the fall of 1980, entitled *Site Visitor's Handbook*. The text of the handbook outlines the accreditation process as a whole and provides detailed guidance for the preparation for, the conduct of, and the reporting of site visits. The several appendices include the two governing documents: (a) the new procedures, which were adopted by the Board of Directors in June 1980, and recommended to the Council of Representatives for its approval in September 1980, and (b) the 1979–80 criteria, together with the report of the task force that drafted them. Also included among the appendices are implementing documents: guidance for the preparation of applications and for annual reports, suggested schedule for site visits, and a check list of the criteria for use by site visitors. These implementing documents and the text of the handbook were approved by the Education and Training Board in May, 1980.

The principal objective of the accreditation process, as outlined in the handbook, is to provide for a systematic appraisal of a program already accredited or applying for accreditation, in terms of the criteria, with the exercise of fair play and due process throughout the entire operation of the program.

There are two general principles fundamental to the operation of the accreditation program. The first is that the burden of proof of compliance with the criteria rests with the program and is demonstrated by the careful preparation of an application and successive annual reports and by the open reception of the site visitors to all facets of the program. In essence, the program needs to respond to the implied question: "Why should the Committee on Accreditation act favorably on my program?" The second objective is that a high degree of considered, professional judgment is required in the review of applications, the conduct and reporting of site visits, and in the committee deliberations. While the committee seeks information on the degree of compliance by the program with each of the several criteria, there is no numerical summation of "scores" on each criterion that must exceed a stated minimum for accreditation. However, there are some criterion statements that contain the words "must" or "shall," noncompliance with which would place a program in jeopardy. This is particularly true of those in Section I, "Institutional Settings." In the final analysis, initial or continued accreditation is determined by a global, professional judgment of the committee on the program as a whole.

The procedures set forth the categories and duration of accreditation, the composition, election, and functions of the Committee on Accreditation (elected by the Education and Training Board), and the kinds of decisions it makes, the process of applying for accreditation, the function of the site visit, mechanisms by which the committee handles complaints about an accredited program, procedures for appealing a decision of the committee, the financial support of the accreditation program and the confidentiality of accreditation records. It is believed that these procedures provide for fair play and due process and will promote a clear understanding of the accreditation process by all concerned. The procedures have been approved by COPA and by the Division of Eligibility and Agency Evaluation of the U.S. Department of Education and are not expected to change substantially over the years.

The 1979-80 Criteria for Accreditation

Unlike the accreditation procedures, the accreditation criteria are subject to revision over the years as the scientific bases of psychology become more comprehensive and new professional techniques and modes of practice develop. As reported by the task force which drafted the 1979-80 criteria, work began with a review of the existing (1973) criteria in relation to the ideas expressed in the Vail conference (Korman, 1976) and "consideration of changes in the criteria appropriate to the emerging professional schools of psychology, whether in universities or organized as independent institutions of higher education." The task force received input from many groups within the governance structure of the APA and from members by letter or in open forums at APA conventions. The criteria were intended for use only with programs in clinical, counseling and school psychology, and the "combined professional program." The task force made a number of general comments about the new criteria under the following headings:

1. *Generality vs. Specificity.* The criteria attempt to show a balance between precise operational language and "guiding principles," leaving to the Committee on Accreditation the preparation of an interpretive handbook.
2. *Boulder Model and the Emergence of the Practitioner Model.* The cri-

teria attempt to reflect an increasing recognition and acceptance of the professional model but are designed to apply to both models. "Programs will be evaluated in terms of the degree to which they meet the goals set within the educational model identified."
3. *Psy.D./Ph.D.* The criteria do not favor one degree over the other.
4. *Human Rights.* The task force received a great deal of input on this topic and devoted much attention to it. Section II of the criteria affirms the significance of human rights and reflects the existing policy statements of the APA as they focus on an educational system.
5. *The Core Curriculum.* Recognizing that the experiences of credentialing and licensing boards have pointed to the need to sharpen the basic definition of what constitutes a psychology program, a number of core topics are identified in Section III, C, in which all students must demonstrate proficiency.

It should be noted that the 1979-80 criteria, like those which preceded it, are *process* rather than *outcome* or *product* criteria. The criteria concern the nature of the educational process and those faculty and students involved in it. They do not attempt, at least in a direct way, to evaluate the program in terms of the professional proficiency of the graduates. The validity of the criteria is, therefore, dependent on the judgment of the drafters that programs which provide the kinds of educational processes described in the criteria will turn out competent professionals. While student work, such as dissertations, are often examined by site visitors, the programs are not judged primarily on the basis of individual performances of students or graduates. Were there reliable and valid means for objectively assessing professional proficiency that could be used without undue cost in time and money, programs could be evaluated solely on the basis of their products regardless of the several training processes by which they were produced. Since such assessment procedures are not likely to be available in the near future, if ever, accreditation of professional psychology programs will continue to depend on process criteria.

The 1979-80 criteria may be said to represent a number of dimensions along which programs may vary. The major dimensions are grouped under seven headings—headings which would apply as well to programs other than psychology and at various educational levels. These major sections of the criteria, designated by roman numerals, are:

    I. Institutional Settings
   II. Cultural and Individual Differences
  III. Training Models and Curricula

IV. Faculty
V. Students
VI. Facilities
VII. Practicum and Internship Training

Within each of these sections are both statements of general principles and some rather specific requirements, each of which might be met in more than one way or to varying degrees. Thus, each of the individual criteria may be regarded as the identification of an important characteristic or dimension along which a particular program would take some value. In only a few cases is the exact required value specified. For example, in section VI on facilities, a number of "dimensions" of facilities (classroom, library, research space, etc.) are identified under the general requirement that they be "adequate." What constitutes adequacy, especially in light of the unique setting of a particular program, is left to the professional judgment of the site visitors and the committee.

As the committee gains experience with the new criteria, information will be accumulated about the various ways in which different programs meet the several criteria and at what points along the dimensions identified by the criteria the several programs seem to lie. Such data will be obtained from study of the annual reports prepared by accredited programs and from the reports of site visits to accredited and applying programs and the programs' responses to these reports. Results of these studies will be aggregated to show the range of compliance among programs and indices of central tendencies of both a quantitative and qualitative nature. Such information, while not intended for the development of rigid standards, will be helpful in applying the criteria in the future. A significant beginning on the accumulation of this information should occur during academic year 1980–81.

Another characteristic of the criteria is their generic nature. Although they are designed as a tool for assessing programs in three psychological specialties, they are much more specific about the nature of the curriculum in general psychology, where several specific areas of required competence are specified, than they are with respect to specialty training. For example, part of Criterion III C states that students must demonstrate compliance in the biological, cognitive-affective, and social bases of behavior and individual behavior, while III D lists specific skills required for competent professional functioning (psychodiagnosis, psychological assessment, intervention procedures, etc.) but does not differentiate between skills uniquely required of clinical, counseling, or school psychologists.

New Challenges for the Accreditation Program

There are several challenges to which the APA accreditation program must respond over the next several years. The first is a continuing challenge, one which confronts every accrediting commission. It is to maintain the criteria used by that commission near the cutting edge of the profession for which its accredited programs train students. Advances are constantly being made in the science of psychology and in its professional practice. As these new developments are evaluated and become available in pedagogical format, they will be adopted by quality training programs. Soon thereafter, they should be reflected in the accreditation criteria so that the general level of preparation for the professional across the country will be continuously upgraded. Improved techniques of teaching and learning, for use in both the classroom and the clinic, should also be considered for inclusion in revision of the criteria. As stated in the report of the task force that drafted the current APA criteria: "A procedure must be established to assure the viability of the accreditation system and its relevance to the profession and public."

A second challenge to the accreditation program is the refinement of criteria which will apply uniquely to each of the current and emerging specialties within the profession. (Resolution 5, adopted by the Virginia Beach conference, makes the same point.) Building on the sound base of the generic portion of current criteria, which provide for a common scientific basis for all specialties, criteria need to be developed to insure preparation of students in the unique knowledge and skills of each specialty. The task for accreditation cannot be accomplished until there is further refinement and agreement on the definition of each specialty. The task must be accomplished if the public is to be assured that a particular specialist in psychology will be able, in fact, to perform in a manner defined as that specialty.

A system for designating graduate programs which are properly classified as psychology is now under development and testing, by a special APA task force. As part of the planning, the proper relationship and articulation between accreditation and designation needs to be worked out. Since designation is being conceptualized primarily in generic terms, it may be that a proper articulation will be between the generic aspects of designation and the specialty aspects of accreditation. Another linkage may be along dimensions of depth, richness and quality of the generic, core aspects of programs. Defining this relationship constitutes a third challenge to the accreditation program.

A fourth challenge is presented by the rapid development of professional schools, particularly those outside a university system. Should there be two sets of criteria: one for traditional programs in university departments of psychology and another for professional schools? Should both programs lead to the same degree? Were usable measures of the proficiency of graduates available, by which the output of different kinds of programs from different settings could be measured, accreditation criteria could shift from a process to a product orientation. If a program were evaluated primarily or exclusively in terms of the professional competence of its graduates, it would be of little concern to the accrediting body by what training program the graduates acquired their knowledge and skills. However, it will be some time, if ever, before such individual assessment procedures become available for general use. Until then, process criteria, which are devised from the experience and judgment of professional trainers, will continue to be used.

Finally the fact that current APA criteria apply equally to the Ph.D., the Psy.D., and the Ed.D. degrees leaves something to be desired. For clarification in the minds of the public, if for no other reason, the scope and content of programs leading to these degrees should be defined and differentiated and these distinctions eventually reflected in the criteria for accreditation.

Note

1. The views expressed in this chapter are those of the author and not necessarily those of the governance structure of the APA.

References

American Psychological Association. *Accreditation procedures and criteria.* Washington, D. C.: American Psychological Asociation, 1973.

American Psychological Association, Office of Accreditation. *Site visitor's handbook.* Washington, D.C.: American Psychological Association, periodically revised.

American Psychological Association Committee on Training in Clinical Psychology. Standards for practicum training in clinical psychology: Tentative recommendations. *American Psychologist,* 1950, *4,* 594-609.

American Psychological Association. *Criteria for accreditation of doctoral programs and internships in professional psychology.* (Xerox) Washington, D.C.: American Psychological Association, 1980.

Committee on Counselor Training, Division of Counseling Guidance, American Psychological Association. The practicum training of counseling psychologists. *American Psychologist,* 1952, *6,* 182-88.

Committee on Training in Clinical Psychology. Recommended graduate training program in clinical psychology. *American Psychologist,* 1947, *1,* 539-58.

Education and Training Board, American Psychological Association. Criteria for evaluating training programs in clinical or in counseling psychology. *American Psychologist,* 1958, *11,* 59-60.

Goodstein, L. D. & Ross, S. Accreditation of graduate programs in psychology: An analysis. *American Psychologist,* 1966, *21,* 218-23.

Harris, S. S. (Ed.). *1979-80 accredited institutions of postsecondary education.* Washington, D. C.: Council on Postsecondary Accreditation, 1979.

Hoch, E. L., Ross, A. D., & Winder, C. L. (Eds.) *Professional preparation of clinical psychologists.* (Chicago conference), Washington, D. C.: American Psychological Association, 1966.

Korman, M. (Ed.). *Levels and patterns of professional training in psychology.* (Vail conference), Washington, D. C.: American Psychological Association, 1976.

Peterson, D. C. (Ed.). *1980-82: A guide to recognized accrediting agencies.* Washington, D. C.: Council on postsecondary accreditation, 1980.

Raimy, V. (Ed.). *Training in clinical psychology.* New York: Prentice-Hall, 1950.

Roe, A., Gustad, J. W., Moore, B. V., Ross, S., & Skodak, M. (Eds.). *Graduate education in psychology.* (Miami conference), Washington, D. C.: American Psychological Association, 1959.

Ross, L. W., Craven, W. J., Jr., Green, Y. W., & Hansley, M. W. (Eds.). *Accredited postsecondary institutions and programs.* Washington, D. C., U. S. Department of Health, Education, and Welfare, 1979.

Strother, C. R. (Ed.). *Psychology and mental health: A report of the institute on education and training for psychological contributions to mental health.* Held at Stanford University, August 1955. Washington, D. C.: American Psychological Association, 1956.

PART C
Program Models

CHAPTER 8

The Freestanding School of Professional Psychology: Current and Future Status

Arthur Kovacs
California School of Professional Psychology

The freestanding school of professional psychology began in California wherein it has continued to grow, though with a number of difficulties, and from which it has extended both northward and eastward. At the time of the Virginia Beach conference there were 15 such independent institutions. By 1980, this number had grown to 21, of which 11 were neither accredited nor a candidate for accreditation by a regional accrediting body. It was the freestanding school model which, as Neill Watson notes in the concluding chapter, provoked the greatest concern of all the issues raised at the Virginia Beach conference, as it has continued to do subsequently.

In the present chapter Dr. Kovacs traces the development of the California School of Professional Psychology, and the special and serious problems the school has faced as it has sought recognition and acceptance as a freestanding institution committed to the provision of quality education in professional psychology. This chapter is especially important for it illustrates the sorts of problems that other dedicated freestanding schools are likely to encounter in their attempts to develop quality professional programming. Despite these serious problems, however, Kovacs remains enthusiastic about the promise and the significance of those freestanding schools which have the flexibility and enthusiasm to adjust to the changing needs of the future education of professional psychologists and the dedication to remain true to the commitment to excellence in this education.

In this presentation I shall describe the experience of the California School of Professional Psychology (CSPP), and in particular the Los Angeles campus, to illustrate some issues that confront freestanding schools of professional psychology. Before doing so, however, it is important to describe the school and some of its history.

The CSPP is now in its tenth academic year. The school has four campuses: the Fresno campus houses approximately 110 students; the

San Diego and San Francisco campuses house approximately 220 students each; and the Los Angeles campus has 260 students in residence; a total of about 810 students. This makes the CSPP the largest professional psychology training institution in the nation. We project that at our present size we will be granting about 180 new doctorates (Ph.D.s) each year.

The school was founded in 1969 with a loan of five thousand dollars from the California State Psychological Association. At the present time, the school's endowment is in excess of 1.4 million dollars and it owns permanent campuses at Berkeley and Fresno. The Los Angeles and San Diego campuses currently are leased but within the next few years these two campuses also will purchase their own space and plants. The school has managed this growth and reached its current size solely by relying on two resources: the use of volunteer help in its beginning years, and its ability to attract and stimulate students who have provided the necessary tuition dollars.

The school is chartered by the state of California as a nonprofit freestanding educational institution. It is governed by a 32-person Board of Trustees, each of whom serves a staggered three-year term. The 32 persons are divided among the following constituencies: 16 of the trustees are elected by the state psychological association, thus ensuring responsiveness on the part of the school to the evolution of the profession; eight members of the Board of Trustees are public members elected by the state psychological association following nomination by a committee of the Board of Trustees; four of the trustees are elected by the faculties of the four campuses and four of the trustees are elected by the students. It is the responsibility of the Board of Trustees to set policy for all of the campuses. In addition, the board hires the president, and upon nomination of the president, appoints the four campus deans. In addition to policy setting, the board approves budgets and oversees the development of the school. Academic policy reaches the board only after review by or recommendation from the faculty of the four campuses.

There is no faculty tenure within the institution. Each campus dean, on recommendation from his/her faculty hiring committee, is empowered to let faculty contracts for lengths of one, two, or three years. The longest faculty contract that exists in the institution is a five-year contract. Each faculty member becomes eligible for five-year contracts after approximately four to six years of service. Five-year contracts must be approved by the Board of Trustees because such contracts represent significant long-term indebtedness on the part of the institution.

About three-quarters of the monies allocated to faculty at each campus are spent on core faculty. (The core faculty comprises those individuals whose contracts call for them to be on campus from one-half to full-time but also contain provisions for adequate release time to pursue some off-campus professional activity.) Core faculty teach about half the courses of the curriculum, manage campus governments, staff faculty committees, supervise student dissertations, and participate in the admissions and advisory process. The other quarter of the faculty budget is spent on the hiring of adjunct faculty; these persons come to campus to teach a specific course or courses. Adjunct faculty teach approximately 50 percent of the offerings in the curriculum. At the Los Angeles campus, for example, there are about one hundred adjunct faculty in residence during the entire academic year.

The curricular model pursued by the CSPP is the professional-scientist model. At the present time, the school is continuing to grant the Ph.D. rather than the Psy.D. and has put together a curriculum that places heavy emphasis on the traditional core courses of scientific psychology. On the professional side, students are exposed to a mixture of theoretical and professional courses and seminars coupled with distributed practica for the first two years and then an internship during the last two years. In the first year, the students are provided with practicum experience involving about 10 to 12 hours a week. During the second year, this practicum requirement occupies about 15 hours each week and during the third and fourth years, students spend about 20 hours each week in internship settings.

The four campuses pursue a school-wide core curriculum. This core takes up about two-thirds of the total course units required of students in the program. Each campus has autonomy to experiment with individualized sequences, to develop programs with special emphases, and to develop their unique resources within the remaining noncore course structure. The academic package consists of three mandatory trimesters a year with 14 weeks in each trimester. All students must be in full-time residency. There are no part-time programs available. The current tuition is $5,445 for the academic year, and it is expected that this figure will increase approximately 11 percent during the next academic year.

The school has attracted students from a wide variety of geographic locations. Forty-four percent of the students come from outside California, and a significant number of these come from foreign countries. Fifty-six percent of the students are female. The students also tend to be older than that traditionally found in graduate programs in psychology. The average age of our incoming students is 29 years, with the range being from 22 to about 60 years.

All four of the CSPP campuses are accredited by the Western Association of Schools and Colleges and each is committed to achieving accreditation from the American Psychological Association (APA). At this point, the Los Angeles campus has received APA accreditation and the San Diego campus is awaiting the outcome of its APA accreditation team visit.

To date, our alumni have fared particularly well in the market place. Within six months of graduation, approximately 96 percent of the students in each of the graduating classes have found relevant employment within psychology.

For those of us who have participated in the development of the CSPP, it has often felt as if we were riding on some avalanche that we had unleashed that would settle in unforeseen and foreseeable places. Despite my enthusiasm, I want to assure you that the problematic tensions which have surrounded these activities have been equally as awesome as the accomplishments. I wish now to turn to the kinds of issues and concerns which currently characterize the CSPP, for I believe that these issues and concerns will be the kinds of concerns which any freestanding school of professional psychology will experience as it seeks to develop.

The early period of rapid expansion and successive achievements is now tapering off. The CSPP currently is laboring on a plateau confronting problems which defy easy solutions and struggling to find new kinds of structures and new energies with which to attack these various problems. Perhaps the most basic problem confronting the school involves the problem of dollar shortages. Because it is a freestanding school, there are all kinds of things for which the CSPP must pay that are available to other programs affiliated with universities. We have to maintain our own business office, our own registrar, our own library, and our own physical plant. All of these things drain about one-third of the tuition dollars. In addition, of course, inflation has been running at a very rapid rate and there is concern that the CSPP may be forced, since it depends entirely on tuition, to price itself out of the market. Ironically, the success of the school has stimulated psychologists in many other parts of the nation to develop professional training programs which now begin to compete with us for applicants. If it is to keep its fiscal solvency, the CSPP must continue to compete successfully in the national applicant forum. The reliance on tuition dollars also requires that the school offer very large courses. But such course offerings provoke an interesting contradiction. While at one time the CSPP was the darling of the profession of psychology in California, many of our professional colleagues now view us with some suspicion and mistrust. We are questioned constantly about the size of our campuses, and we come under attack for training so many psychologists who are perceived as potentially flooding an already crowded job market. While there are no hard data available to indicate that the existence of the school is having a deleterious effect on the profession in California, feelings tend to run high. We have not succeeded in persuading our colleagues of the wisdom of our mission even though we can present evidence to them that our graduates do not wind up on the unemployment lines, but indeed find adequate employment in psychology. The debate is a highly emotional one and probably not very subject to rational considerations.

We are also in trouble at the present time because there has been a gradual drying up of adequate field placement opportunities for students in the four cities in which our campuses are located. Community agencies, of course, are experiencing the same kinds of difficulties in funding. Whereas once, for example, we could rely upon about $500,000 worth of paid field placements for our students in the greater Los Angeles area, this figure has steadily declined over the last five years to the point where now we can depend upon only about $125,000 a year. In addition, the most competent staff in many of the field placement agencies have been leaving because of the funding cutbacks at the county, state, and national levels. The resulting confusion leaves fewer field placements providing good quality training for our students. As a result, we have had to seek creative solutions including the establishment of our own psychological services center. But the vicious circle spirals, for it is as hard for us to find sufficient capital for our own psychological services center as it is for the agencies in the community to secure the fiscal resources necessary for their effective operations. We have managed to plunge forward, however, and our services center has come into being in a limited way. At the present time, this center provides outpatient psychotherapy to the local community. It also has a contract with a local community college to provide mental health services on site at that college and, in addition, we are running a juvenile drug diversion program for the Los Angeles County Sheriff's Department. Approximately 10 percent of the students of the CSPP Los Angeles campus will spend at least one of their years in residency at one of the programs of the services center. But much more help is needed, for we would like the service center to grow and to truly pioneer in the delivery of both direct and indirect services of the kind that we think would make an innovative professional school proud of its creativity. At the present time, our other three campuses also are struggling to establish their psychological service centers.

Just how we will manage to aid the future development of psychological services centers is uncertain. What is certain, however, is that the task will be arduous. We have begun to explore the possibility of mounting a variety of continuing education experiences for the profession, for related health and mental health professionals, and for the general public. While these efforts will continue, we do not have the kind of visibility with the general public and with other professionals that makes audiences very easy to come by, and we also are plagued by the absence of adequate auditorium space on our campuses. I think that our commitment to continuing education is going to mimic the history of our establishment of a psychological services center. We will begin to experiment with a variety of small programs, and we will have to extract boot-strap capital out of our own limited resources as we gradually develop a market and slowly expand the kinds of offerings we would like to promote until such a time as continuing education generates the supplemental income necessary to aid further development of the basic campus program itself.

Another factor limiting the school's fiscal integrity is that it is a relatively new institution, whereby it is quite difficult to attract extramural grants and gifts. It will take some time before foundations and public agencies will have come to know and esteem the school's contributions in a fashion that will make them willing to provide funding for our continued development. With the APA accreditation of the Los Angeles campus, the prospects of both VA internships and NIMH predoctoral fellowships for our students can be realized.

Despite the fiscal limitations, the CSPP continues to thrive and survive on the idealism of the professionals who constitute its working faculties. Most of those who teach in the institution do so because they are committed to its ideals and because they see in it an important social experiment that will affect profoundly the future of our profession. The faculty work load in the institution is much greater than is true in the more traditional schools. A full-time equivalent teaching load on most CSPP campuses varies between 30 and 36 units spaced over an academic year. In addition to teaching, each faculty member is expected to chair three or four dissertations, to participate in governance, and to do student advisement, admissions, and the other kinds of functions that faculty in any institution are expected to carry out. The fringe benefits for faculty are quite minimal. While there is a health plan and a self-contributing retirement program, no travel funds or sabbaticals are available to CSPP faculty, and there is only limited support staff and teaching assistant help to conduct the academic programs. While faculty salaries are competitive with those paid to faculties in liberal arts institutions in California, they are not competitive with what experienced professional psychologists can earn in settings other than those provided by academic institutions. I believe that the only reason that CSPP is able to attract and hold a capable cadre of committed faculty members is that it provides such faculty with adequate release time to carry on off-campus professional activities.

The CSPP campuses also are struggling with complex problems of faculty building. In the beginning, the institution was staffed by volunteers who came forward to teach particular courses. Most of these people tended to be practicing psychologists, psychologists from other academic institutions or from field placement agencies, who believed in the CSPP concept and who were willing to donate a few hours a week of instruction in order to aid the struggling school as it launched itself into the first years of operation. From this cadre of volunteer faculty slowly emerged a group of persons who were more committed to the institution. These individuals looked to the institution to provide them with a home and a base for the further prosecution of their own professional careers. Since our curriculum has been evolving over the years, and since we have maintained steadfastly that we desire to be a Ph.D. degree-granting institution, we also have been confronted with the responsibility for attracting to the core faculty psychologists who were other than practitioners. It has been necessary to recruit and to attract social psychologists, experimental psychologists, development psychologists, and others to be part of the educational process of the institution. As we have evolved over these first ten years, we have experienced considerable faculty turnover and faculty recruitment. This has produced some degree of instability and anxiety on the part of the professionals who staff the program. Faculty review committees and the administration are confronting constantly the issue of how to go about faculty building and attracting quality professional staff in a fashion that permits the turnover of less capable members of the faculty and, at the same time, does not generate such anxiety among all members of the campus community that the atmosphere of the program becomes unbearable for all participants. This is not an easy task, and there have been times when one or another of the four campuses have suffered because of some excess in zeal in faculty building.

Difficulties in securing an adequate funding base for the school also have resulted in a turning away from what was a very precious initial part of the dream of the CSPP. The school emerged in the late 1960s, not only to provide a home in which professional psychologists would train future generations of professional psychologists but, in a very idealistic way, there was a desire on the part of the State Psychological Association in California to develop an instrumentality that would recruit and attract many more minority group students into the field of psychology. Economic realities, however, have forced us to develop a school with very expensive tuition and schools with very expensive tuition find it especially hard to recruit and maintain minority group members in residency. CSPP attempts to address the issue, in part, by committing three percent of its tuition resources in direct aid to its own student body. Since our annual budget is now approaching three and a half million dollars, this means that in excess of $100,000 is available on the four campuses for the support of needy students. This amount, however, only represents tuition scholarships for about 20 students out of a total student body of 810. It will not be before some years hence, when the institution has established a funding base that is much broader than the direct tuition dollars paid by its student bodies, that an adequate job of minority re-cruitment and education at CSPP will be possible.

There are at least two new trends in the development of the California School of Professional Psychology that are attempts to solve the various problems I have outlined. The first of these attempts is based on an alternation of the perceptions about the kinds of senior administrators appropriate for the running of the institution. Following the retirement of our founding president, Nicholas A. Cummings, the Board of Trustees came to the conclusion that the appropriate qualifications for the presi-dent of the institution did not necessarily involve those of a professional psychologist. It was the perception of the board that the president needed to be a person with established credentials in relating to funding agencies and governmental instrumentalities. One who might address creatively development issues while delegating to the deans and the fac-ulties on the four campuses the responsibility for the management of the academic program. John R. O'Neil, who formerly had been vice presi-dent for community relations at Mills College in California, was hired as the second president of the institution. Similarly, when I retired as dean of the Los Angeles campus, the faculty search committee made a recom-mendation that the campus retain the services of Abbott Kaplan to be that campus' second dean. Dr. Kaplan has particular expertise as an academic administrator. Before coming to Los Angeles to be responsible for our campus, he had been president of the State University of New York at Purchase. While not a psychologist, Dr. Kaplan's credentials as a school administrator and his capabilities at establishing good community relationships and effective management strategies for the campus are impeccable. I believe that these trends represent the directions to be followed by any freestanding institution such as the CSPP. It will be professional psychologists who will take the responsibility for building the institution, but as such schools evolve, their management must be turned over to professional administrators and to persons who can secure the kinds of extramural funding and develop the kinds of community relationships that professional psychologists do not necessarily know how to go about doing.

The second set of notions for improving the solidity of the CSPP base involves a serious and thoughtful response to recommendations which recently have been made to the institution by the Western Association of Schools and Colleges. Site visitors consistently have stated that we ought to explore the possibility of cooperative arrangements with other academic programs in the areas in which the CSPP campuses are located. In the months ahead, a series of dialogues will be undertaken between the CSPP campuses and various campuses of the State College System together with private institutions such as Claremont College and the California Institute of Technology. In these discussions we will explore possibilities of joint degree programs and of sharing facilities such as library holdings, general space, laboratory space, instructional aids, computer facilities, and teaching equipment. Perhaps in the future, the CSPP will cease to be a freestanding university and will merge with one or more of the more established institutions of higher education. Even before we consider such possibilities, however, it may prove to be fruitful to undertake those kinds of negotiations aimed at preventing duplication and establishing cost-effective, sensible, and imminently feasible cooperative arrangements. With university enrollments declining slowly within the state, it would make excellent sense to secure the optimum benefit from the kinds of facilities and resources that various programs hold and to develop some consortium arrangements for the benefit of the students at several different institutions of higher education.

It also is my sense that CSPP must soon reconsider the kinds of academic and curriculum packaging that it has put together. To repeat what I noted earlier, for ten years the school has run a mandatory trimester program throughout its academic year and it has required that students be in full-time residency taking an average of 15 units per trimester. This means that there are only two weeks vacation at Christmas time, two weeks in the spring, and only about five weeks each summer. Because of the heavy teaching load on faculty, because of the serious demands made on students in terms of academic course work on campus, and because of the complexities of commuting to practica and field placement agencies, with the many hours of work that these entail each week, each year the school seems to be in the grip of serious student and faculty "burn out." At several predictable points during the academic year, both the instructional staff and the student body seem to get quite depressed and demoralized, ridden with fatigue and unable to exert the optimal kinds of energy required for reasonable learning. Many different plans are being discussed on the four campuses for relieving these kinds of pressures. One of the most popular plans involves transforming the program into a five-year, two-semester program. This would allow for a lengthy summer vacation for students and staff alike, it would represent a reduction of one-third in faculty work load, and it would permit students either simply to enjoy the freedom of a summer vacation or, for those who find it difficult to meet the high cost of tuition, to obtain work during the summer period. Under such a system, the summer periods probably would be used for remedial courses for students in difficulty and for the mounting of continuing education experiences for the profession and the public.

Let me close this section on the current problems which CSPP faces at this period of its evolution by noting several additional difficulties brought about by the fact that we have come into existence as a freestanding institution. Because we were one of the first professional schools of psychology, and because we are not affiliated with any other academic institution, we have been subjected to an incredible array of site visits. In the first nine years of our existence, for example, we received 45 such visits. Sixteen of these were from the Western Association of Schools and Colleges as we struggled to receive our regional accreditation, 12 of these were from the Department of Education of the state of California that had to make decisions relative to whether or not we would be granted the right to confer degrees within the state, eight visits have come from APA's Office of Minority Fellowships, six visits were mounted by the National Institute of Mental Health in response to various applications for training funds, and three visits have been held by various site visiting teams from the APA's Committee on Accreditation. It sometimes feels as if each of the campuses is either in the middle of preparing for a site visit, having a site visit, or recovering from a site visit. I believe that this experience will be true for the other programs that choose to become freestanding institutions.

One of the consequences of such a heavy and concentrated dose of site visiting activity is that any new freestanding program must be prepared to deal with an array of contradictions. Each site visiting team received by a campus has its own particular perspectives on the strengths and weaknesses of the program as the visit unfolds. Each site visiting team makes a series of recommendations about what needs to be improved or what needs to be modified before the time of the next visit. A new and developing program often will find itself caught in a variety of contradictory recommendations. It is hard to say what the answer to this dilemma is, but other programs that are going to follow CSPP's example will find themselves faced with the creative challenge of reconciling the sometimes conflicting perspectives of visitors sent by the state, the regional accrediting bodies, various funding sources, and the APA. It seems, at this point in the development of American psychology, that there simply is no clear and unifying vision of what a good professional psychology training program ought to be. Site visitors, therefore, tend to make recommendations in line with their own particular idiosyncratic perspectives.

As an evolving freestanding school, CSPP has also faced an additional problem. Since initially we had no reputation, no visibility, and no credibility, a great deal of staff and professional time had to be put into liaison and dialogue with a variety of bureaucratic organizations that would have impact on the future of our alumni. It is hard to estimate how much time has been committed by school personnel communicating with representatives of licensing boards in fifty states in the nation, with civil service examiners at the municipal, county, and state levels across the country, and with prospective employers of our graduates. We have needed to explain to all of these people what CSPP is, how it was founded, and what credentials it has acquired at various points in its evolution. We have had to persuade these persons to evaluate our products on their merits. I feel we have been very successful in responding to such an onerous challenge, but any program that is going to follow CSPP's history also is going to have to be prepared to spend the necessary time to carry on the conversations which will accomplish these tasks.

But what of the future? As I think about how far we have come, and I reflect about the very great challenges the institution still faces, I am struck also by what I believe will be a very necessary self-transcendence in which the CSPP will have to engage in the years ahead. The largest number of students who apply for admission to our program seem to manifest the phenomenon that can only be described as a kind of cultural lag. Most of them have had some brush with professional psychology. For a significant number of them, this has occurred through having undergone psychotherapy. Many people hope to enter the institution to be trained in the skills, the perspectives, and the models that have existed over the last decade or so of what a psychologist is. But if there is anything sure about our unique profession, it is that we are a profession in a state of profound flux. Certainly, we attempt to meet the desires of our students to be well trained in the techniques of individual and group assessment, and individual and group psychotherapy. In addition to providing training to our students to develop the traditional skills, we seek to push our students to develop their capabilities as scientists. Yet, while many of our students are willing to do this, research is not something which they find particularly exciting. I do not believe that CSPP, nor professional schools of psychology anywhere, can continue to flourish if they aim to train students primarily in the techniques of assessment and psychotherapy. Too many social developments, already clearly on the horizon, suggest that a program oriented primarily for training in these particular kinds of skills and attitudes is likely to be training for obsolescence.

Social developments here in California make it obvious that professional psychology must become more than simply a preparation for a career in the delivery of direct services. Within this state, we have witnessed the creation of a licensed profession known as marriage, family, and child counseling. This profession consists of persons trained at the masters level who may apply for an appropriate credential from the state. Upon passing the necessary examination, they are granted a license to enter private practice to function as marriage, family, and child counselors. For those of you who are not aware of the scope of this phenomenon, let me note that at the present time approximately 4,000 such persons are applying for the examination each year! I believe that the social development represented by the establishment of such a profession in California—and California tends to be the laboratory for all kinds of social experiments—will spread across the country. We recently have witnessed a battle, for example, in Texas over the establishment of a profession known as "social psychotherapy." Be that as it may, there is every likelihood that the delivery of direct remedial services to individuals and to groups may be delegated downwards from doctoral level professionals to those trained at the masters level and appropriately credentialed within the various states.

Somewhere in the future, when inflation, economic circumstances, and political realities allow, this country will enact some form of national health care legislation. Due to the efforts of the Association for the Advancement of Psychology, and our colleagues around the nation who have actively attempted to make psychology's case known in forums where this would count, I believe that there is a very strong likelihood that psychology will be included as an autonomous profession delivering health care services within proposed national health legislation. When this happens, there are simply not going to be enough persons trained in the delivery of professional psychological services at the doctoral level to go around. I believe that we will have to rely upon paraprofessionals to render the largest portion of direct human services or the system will collapse. At the CSPP, we are expanding our horizons and modifying our curriculum slowly as our experience accumulates. We believe that the future of our graduates will be guaranteed best not by training them to do individual assessment or individual and group psychotherapy, but in providing them with a set of generic skills that will allow them to capitalize on such future professional developments. We intend to alter our curriculum to provide our students an opportunity to develop at least journeyperson ability in such alternate, indirect skills as consultation, teaching, supervision of other mental health professionals, program evaluation, administration, and grantsmanship.

It is our contention that the future careers of doctoral level professional psychologists will involve a large proportion of time spent in these kinds of activities. I believe that professional training programs across the country need to consider these perspectives. I believe we bear a special responsibility of remaining sensitive to the opportunities and challenges of the social requirements that lie in our immediate future. Those programs that become locked into training students for careers that have existed in the past run the danger of failing to glimpse the kinds of opportunities for which students will need to be prepared. I believe the biggest of these challenges is to ensure that the professional school movement extends beyond training clinical psychologists, into the creative challenge of training a kind of generic professional psychologist who will be able to adapt to the circumstances of the 1980s and beyond.

CHAPTER 9

The Development of a Doctor of Psychology (Psy.D.) Program in a Medical College and Hospital Setting

Clifford M. DeCato
Hahnemann Medical College and Hospital

In this chapter Dr. DeCato describes the development and operation of the Hahnemann Program in Professional Psychology. Perhaps the unique feature of this Doctor of Psychology program is that it is the first and still the only clinical psychology program in a medical school setting. The paper describes the educational philosophy on which the program is based and emphasizes the balance between didactic components and experiential component. The structure and content of the program also are outlined to show the sequence of courses and the relationship of the curriculum and training to the educational objectives. Finally, Dr. De-Cato addresses the advantages and disadvantages which he notes for the program as a consequence of its unique institutional setting.

The initial phases of the Hahnemann psychology program were begun in 1970. This program is unique because it was developed in a medical college and hospital setting. At the very least, the existence of a viable professional psychology program was previously debated only on a theoretical plane.

The Department of Mental Health Sciences is one of the larger departments of Hahnemann Medical College and Hospital. It has several divisions, numerous training programs, and an associated community mental health center. The nature and organization of the Department of Mental Health Sciences and the community mental health center form the primary training resource and set the basic parameters within which the doctoral program functions. Several characteristics of this setting have facilitated the development of a professional psychology program.

Perhaps the foremost resource is the large number of highly qualified professionals in the mental health field who are actively involved in the training programs of the Department of Mental Health Sciences. The total faculty and staff number approximately 300. Following a medical school tradition, many practicing professionals give some time for teaching and supervising. These part-time faculty swell the total number of professionals engaged in giving some form of training to several hundred. All major mental health disciplines are represented within this faculty.

The department has functioned in an interdisciplinary fashion for many years and has a strong philosophical commitment to the proposition that it is to the benefit of the mental health field and the consuming public for professionals to share knowledge and work closely together. The teaching faculty are practicing clinicians who lend credence and relevance to the course work and provide working models for the students. The students are treated with respect; regarded as professionals in training, soon to be colleagues of the staff. This facilitates the development of a professional identity and the incorporation of professional values and modes of conduct.

The Hahnemann Community Mental Health Center is a large urban mental health and mental retardation center serving an inner city area of Philadelphia of approximately 200,000 people. The catchment area contains large minority groups (Black and Puerto Rican), underserved, and socioeconomically deprived populations. In 1977 the department began providing mental health services in the Philadelphia prisons. The services collectively provided by the Hahnemann Community Mental Health Center and specialized programs associated with Hahnemann cover a full range of service modalities in common usage in the mental health field today. Treatment approaches range from preventive programs targeted for high risk preschool children to in- and out-patient services, crisis and emergency services, and consultation and education programs.

General Objectives

The Scholar-Professional

The training atmosphere provides a model that shows respect for the personal dignity and professional maturity of the graduate student. The learning climate promotes open communication between staff and students which establishes a model for the clinical approach to the patient, the patient's family, and the community. The student is provided with a model emphasizing the unfinished state of knowledge and encouraged in an attitude of critical inquest and continuing education. High value is placed simultaneously on developing practical skills and competencies commensurate with the best practices in the field. This combination of scholarship and competence is characterized by the term scholar-practitioner.

Multifaceted Orientation

Students are provided with the opportunity to become familiar with a wide spectrum of information and experience that will make them competent psychologists. Classroom didactic instruction is combined with sequential, graded experiences under supervision covering major theories and modalities current in the mental health field.

Emphasis on Underserved Populations

Emphasis in both didactic course-work and in the clinical experiences is placed on systems and techniques suitable for minority groups, low income populations, social psychology, correctional psychology, school related problems, and other areas of specialized skills and knowledge relevant to underserved populations.

Community Psychology, Consultation, and Education

A major frame of reference assumed throughout the program is the postulate that social-environmental factors are critically important in determining and changing behavior. Social and institutional determinants of human functioning are given equal weight with individual and intra-psychic factors.

Semispecialization

Although the program primarily aims at giving the student a thorough foundation and introduction to basic knowledge and skills, it is recognized that five years is insufficient to achieve equally high degrees of skill in all areas. Beginning in the third year of training, the student is allowed some degree of concentration in areas of his/her interest. The vehicle for this semispecialization is provided by elective courses, internship choices, and individualized readings and research projects which form "tracks." Tracks now in partial or full operation include intervention techniques, diagnostic assessment, family therapy, and neuropsychology.

The Educational Model

The educational model underlying the psychology program at Hahnemann postulates that preparation for entry into professional psychology requires the imparting of knowledge, skills, and attitudes by the program to the person aspiring to enter the field. Knowledge in this model is broadly conceptualized to mean the body of theories, facts, constructs, research, and network of literature surrounding the practice of clinical psychology. Skills are those aspects of the practical application of theories and techniques that are considered to be applied competencies. Attitudes are those aspects of professional identity that include values, ethics, and the spoken and covert guiding principles for appropriate professional conduct.

TABLE 9.1

Schematic Presentation of the Curriculum by Year Sequence Showing Potential Sources for Meeting Program Objectives of the Educational Model

YEAR	*CURRICULUM*		*GOALS*
FIRST YEAR	CORE CURRICULUM	50% didactic 50% practica (2 days)	knowledge skills
SECOND YEAR	CORE CURRICULUM	50% didactic 50% practica (2 days)	knowledge skills
THIRD YEAR	DOCTORAL	50% didactic (3 day internship)	knowledge skills
FOURTH YEAR	DOCTORAL	50% didactic (3 day internship)	knowledge skills
FIFTH YEAR	DOCTORAL	50% didactic plus additional doctoral clinical project (3 day internship)	

Table 9.1 shows how this educational model operates in the Hahnemann psychology program. The total course of training extends over five years. The general sources in the program for meeting each of the three components of the model (knowledge, skills, and attitudes) are indicated.

The assumption is made that applied competencies require extensive supervised practical experiences and that the opportunity for integration of theory and facts with practice is enhanced by having ongoing practical experience concomitant with formal didactic work. Every effort is made to strike an approximately equal balance between the amount of time spent in formal educational pursuits (classes, readings, and so on) and practical applied experiences. This educational model sets as ideal 50 percent time spent in formal instruction and literature preparations and 50 percent time spent in supervised practical clinical experience. Students have practicum experiences from the time they enter the program. For the first two years the practica are two days per week for 10 months each year. Each internship is in one setting for one year. A new setting is assigned each year to insure exposure to a variety of patient populations and clinic settings. For the third, fourth, and fifth years of training the internship is three days per week. The knowledge or scholarship component of training is provided primarily by the didactic aspects of the curriculum. The skill component leading to specific competencies is continuously developed by the supervised internships.

Attitudes are instilled from a variety of sources in the program. The model set by the teaching faculty and by supervisory staff is, of course, a primary source for incorporating a professional identity. Readings and course instruction also stimulate reflection on values relating to patient care, professional roles, and legal-ethical issues in the profession. Attitudes about scholarship are actively promoted by the teaching faculty, many of whom emphasize the unfinished and incomplete nature of knowledge and the need for continuing education. Examples of professional scholarship also are provided by the faculty who engage the students in projects leading to professional publications.

The courses in the core curriculum are closely sequenced. Table 9.2 shows the current sequence of core courses over the first and second years of training. The advanced courses for the third, fourth, and fifth years of training are less closely sequenced than the core courses and are shown in Table 9.3.

Training Procedures

Implementation of the educational model falls into essentially three components: a didactic component including curriculum and faculty, an experiential (internship) component, and an assessment component.

The didactic component consists of classroom instruction and faculty resources. All modalities of instruction common to classroom types of formal learning are used in the program.

TABLE 9.2

Curriculum for First Two Years (Core)

Core I

FIRST QUARTER		SECOND QUARTER		THIRD QUARTER	
Human Development: Intro.	3 cr.	Human Development: Advanced	3 cr.	Clinical Aspects of Child Development	3 cr.
Basic Concepts of Psychological Testing	3 cr.	Psychopathology of Adolescence	3 cr.	Adult Psychopathology	3 cr.
Practicum in Cognitive Functioning & Evaluation	3 cr.	Practicum in Intellectual Functioning	3 cr.	Introduction to Basic Concepts of Research	3 cr.
Basic Concepts of Psychotherapy	3 cr.	Introduction to Individual Dynamic Psychotherapy	3 cr.	Introduction to Projective Techniques	3 cr.
Psychopathology of Childhood	3 cr.	Foundations of Community Psychology	3 cr.	Introduction to Behavior Therapy	2 cr.
Clinic Practicum I	3 cr.	Clinic Practicum I	3 cr.	Clinic Practicum I	3 cr.
				Dialogues in Clinical Practice	3 cr.

Core II

FIRST QUARTER		SECOND QUARTER		THIRD QUARTER	
Introduction to Piaget	3 cr.	Rorschach Interpretation	3 cr.	Adult Development	3 cr.
Introduction to Family Therapy	3 cr.	Introduction to Statistics	3 cr.	Diagnostic Psychological Testing	3 cr.
Rorschach Scoring: Percept-analytic System	3 cr.	Introduction to Group Therapy	3 cr.	Techniques of Child Therapy	3 cr.
Psychology of the Character Disordered Individual	3 cr.	Diagnosis of Learning	3 cr.	Community Consultation & Evaluation	3 cr.
Clinic Practicum II	2 cr.	Theories of Personality	3 cr.	Forensic Psychology: An Introduction	3 cr.
Medical Information	3 cr.	Clinic Practicum II	2 cr.	Clinic Practicum II	3 cr.
Dialogues in Clinical Practice (Elective)	2 cr.	Dialogues in Clinical Practice (Elective)	2 cr.	Dialogues in Clinical Practice	2 cr.

The faculty structure is somewhat different from that found in a typical university setting. Four types of faculty function in the program. First, there is a core faculty consisting of the director and six full-time psychologists. These persons devote full time to administering, instructing, supervising, and providing program consistency, integration, and leadership. The second faculty group comprises full-time psychologists in the Department of Mental Health Sciences who give a regular percentage of their time to teaching, supervising, and committee service in the program. Many of these faculty have been with the program since its beginning and function very much like the core faculty. A third faculty resource is the nonpsychologist faculty who are employed full time in the department (social workers, psychiatrists) who teach courses in their area of practice or give supervision. This faculty epitomizes the interdisciplinary orientation of the program. The fourth faculty group, as is the tradition of other professional programs, consists of a large pool of "clinical" or "adjunct" faculty who are part-time members of the department and whose function primarily is to teach courses in their area of expertise or to give clinical supervision to the psychology interns. The total number of faculty who contribute time to the psychology program is more than 250.

The second component used to implement the educational model involves the internship program. The majority of interns are placed in one or another of the various service units and programs offered by the Hahnemann Community Mental Health Center. However, specialized internship settings such as prison settings, schools for children with learning disabilities, a pediatric psychology unit, a psychosomatic liaison unit, and a variety of in- and outpatient services also are available.

The third component of the model involves assessment of student progress. The program systematically evaluates the students in several ways. Traditional classroom techniques including course examinations, papers, and participation are routinely used as part of didactic instruction. At the end of the second core year, a written qualifying examination is administered covering the content of the core curriculum. In the fourth year, a written comprehensive examination is administered. This examination covers six areas: psychopathology, developmental psychology, diagnostic assessment, intervention techniques, research, and professional ethics. An assessment modeled after the ABPP examination occurs in the final year. A committee of three faculty orally examines the student for three hours. One hour is devoted to diagnostic techniques and includes a sample testing case, either child or adult. One hour is given to examining a verbatim transcript of a therapy session. The third hour is spent examining the person's grasp of professional issues and

TABLE 9.3

Curriculum for Advanced Courses

Advanced III

FIRST QUARTER		SECOND QUARTER		THIRD QUARTER	
Professional Issues and Ethics	3 cr.	Continuous Case Conference: Child	3 cr.	Continuous Case Conference: Dynamic Child	3 cr.
Differential Diagnosis: Child	3 cr.	Seminar in Differential Diagnosis: Child	3 cr.	Neuropsychology: Introduction	3 cr.
Continuous Case Conference: Child	3 cr.	School Psychology	3 cr.	History and Systems	3 cr.
Dissertation Research	3 cr.	Basic Theory of Psychoanalysis	3 cr.	School Consultation	3 cr.
Family Therapy Case Conference	2 cr.	Behavior Therapy Case Conference	2 cr.		
Behavior Therapy Case Conference	2 cr.	Seminar in Human Sexuality	2 cr.		
Seminar on Borderline	2 cr.	Supervision, Staff Training & Consultation	2 cr.		
Development of Communication	2 cr.	Dissertation Research	3 cr.		
Seminar on the Changing Family	2 cr.				
Seminar in Forensic Psychology	2 cr.				

Advanced IV

FIRST QUARTER		SECOND QUARTER		THIRD QUARTER	
Continuous Case Conference: Adult	3 cr.	Continuous Case Conference: Adult	3 cr.	Continuous Case Conference: Adult	3 cr.
Social Psychology	3 cr.	Seminar on Differential Diagnosis: Adult	3 cr.	Seminar on Differential Diagnosis: Adult	3 cr.
Seminar in Differential Diagnosis: Adult	3 cr.	Organizational Psychology	3 cr.	Theories of Learning & Motivation	3 cr.

Dissertation Research	3 cr.
Family Therapy Case Conference	2 cr.
Behavior Therapy Case Conference	2 cr.
Development of Communication	2 cr.
Seminar in Forensic Psychology	2 cr.
Basic Theory of Psychoanalysis	2 cr.

Basic Theory of Psychoanalysis	2 cr.
Behavior Therapy Case Conference	2 cr.
Seminar in Human Sexuality	2 cr.
Supervision, Staff Training & Consultation	2 cr.
Dissertation Research	3 cr.

Advanced V

Diagnostic Case Conference: Adult	3 cr.
Adolescent Case Conference: (Elective)	2 cr.
Seminar on Clinical Problems	2 cr.
Difficult Issues in Differential Diagnosis	2 cr.
Issues in Community Psychology	3 cr.
Family Therapy Case Conference	2 cr.
Behavior Therapy Case Conference	2 cr.
Seminar on Borderline	2 cr.
Development of Communication	2 cr.
Seminar on the Changing Family	3 cr.
Seminar in Forensic Psychology	2 cr.

Diagnostic Case Conference: Adult	3 cr.
Clinical Psychopathology	3 cr.
Continuous Case Conference: Adolescense (Elective)	2 cr.
Dissertation	3 cr.
Seminar on Death & Dying	2 cr.
Supervision, Staff Training & Consultation	2 cr.
Seminar, Theories & Perspectives of Childhood	2 cr.

ethics. Each area is independently assessed for pass or fail. The clinical skills of the student are evaluated periodically throughout the program by supervisors so that corrective measures can be taken early if problems begin to emerge. Finally, in the last year the student is required to complete a clinical dissertation. This project aims at helping the student integrate previous learning and intensify his/her knowledge in an area of interest. This paper is the final exercise in scholarship required in the program.

Admission Procedures

Perhaps the most arduous single task facing the faculty each year is the admission process. The importance of this effort cannot be over-emphasized. No other single task is as crucial to success or failure as the selection of persons with intellectual and personality characteristics that match the program curriculum and objectives.

There are 400-500 applications for between 15-20 position openings in the program each year. Admission is determined by a committee of about ten faculty members. The selections made by this committee receive the approval of the admissions committee of the graduate school before becoming final. Based on our experience with admissions to the program and later successes and failures within the program, four major sources of information have been identified for use in selecting qualified candidates. An experimental scale was developed that incorporated these four types of information into a conception of "graduate ability" using a forced normal curve to rate the factors with approximately equal weight. The first factor may be called "scholastic ability," measured by the Graduate Record Exam (GRE) scores, the Miller Analogies Test (MAT) scores, and an estimated grade point average. This factor yields one composite score to predict the likelihood that the applicant can master the scholarship demands of the program. "Personal reference" value is the second factor. This factor is judged from letters of reference. "Clinical experience" is the third factor. It is judged from autobiographical material, letters from supervisors, and any other information submitted with the application that helps to understand if the applicant has had experience that is relevant, the length of this experience, and the quality of the experience. The final factor considered is "personal attributes" observed during an interview by one or more of the faculty members.

To date we have used the scale only as a screening device and do not have any additional standardization studies. The scale seems to be most helpful in the initial screening process. By providing a rough comparison among applicants, it helps identify those persons who are strongest in three of the four factors, excluding the interview. Use of the scale helps the admissions committee determine the top 25 percent of the applicants who are then offered a personal interview. A final decision is made after the interview.

Finding qualified minority applicants has been quite difficult. The program has an affirmative action policy and has managed to obtain approximately ten percent minority (Black and Hispanic) representation in recent years. However, we were not so fortunate in the early years. This means that some of the advanced classes have an underrepresentation of minorities. We do not use quotas for minorities, but we do take care to identify as many minority applicants as possible and make contact with those who meet general standards. We have contacts with Black associations and colleges with strong Black populations, and we subscribe to the GRE Minority Locator Service.

Program Evaluation

Past evaluations of the program have been conducted in an informal fashion. The program is operated in such a fashion that there is continuous feedback from students, faculty, and associated clinics. Surveys have been conducted periodically to make us aware of the employment settings of the doctoral graduates and the perception of training received by these graduates. We also have received informal feedback from those who have hired our graduates. This information has been used to guide the development of the program and institute changes. We also have solicited critical independent evaluations on two different occasions from the APA Office of Educational Affairs. All these critiques have been used to guide the development of the program. In the fall of 1979, the program received full, five-year APA accreditation.

The educational objective of our program is to produce "scholar-professionals." We believe that there is some evidence available bearing on this issue. Five classes (30 persons) of Doctor of Psychology (Psy.D.) candidates have been graduated as of June 1980. Thus, the fundamental objectives of establishing, developing, and managing a psychology graduate training program in a medical school setting have been attained. A recent survey of program graduates revealed that all were employed in appropriate positions of responsibility in recognized clinics and mental health facilities. Some have already attained substantial responsibilities beyond the staff level. Given the present tight job market, we believe these facts reflect well on the training provided. Informal feedback from the clinics has been generally complimentary. Many of the graduates have achieved licensure in Pennsylvania and/or in New Jersey. Some who are licensed have part-time or full-time private practices and some are in group private practice. These states require boarding examinations covering theoretical and applied areas. This fact is suggestive evidence that our graduates are objectively perceived by independent, critical professionals as meeting standards for practice in the field of psychology.

A concern often voiced in the literature pertaining to professional programs is that such training leads to practitioners devoid of interest in either pursuing or imparting knowledge in the field. This has not been the case. Many of our students have published jointly with faculty and some have books or articles that have been published independently. Of course, the emphasis in these writings is applied, professional, or in some way involved in integrating or demonstrating principles useful in applied work. Nevertheless, we believe that these publications demonstrate the ability of our students to generate ideas and express their competencies at a level commensurate with the expectations for psychology students in general. Since the students are motivated by studying and writing in areas of their interest, we believe that they are inclined, even more than the average clinical student, to seek ways to communicate their work to other professionals.

Teaching and supervising experiences are components of the program. Students are encouraged to teach courses to undergraduates and to students in allied fields (mental health technology students, medical students, nurses). It was expected that some of the students will continue to incorporate some teaching in their work because they have been motivated toward scholarship in the program. One of our recent graduates was hired at the assistant professor level in the tenure track at a well-known college on the Eastern seaboard. Some others, who have settled in the Philadelphia area, have joined the adjunct faculty and continue to do some supervising and teaching. These occurrences suggest that the program has stimulated and maintained motivation for continued learning and participation in scholarship among a substantial number of the graduates.

Advantages and Disadvantages of the Setting

Reviewing the development of the Hahnemann program over the past decade, one can see both advantages and disadvantages for the program as a function of the setting in which it exists. The advantages which we have experienced are several:

1. The faculty and staff involved in teaching and supervising are clearly dedicated to professional practice. They teach what they do, which

provides the students with role models. Moreover, there tends to be little conflict within the faculty concerning the relevance or value of practical professional work or integrating research and teaching with direct delivery of services.

2. Students benefit from the close working alliance between psychological and medical faculty. Practical experience is gained in understanding the concept of team work in mental health services. The psychology students learn to understand and work with a medical perspective while simultaneously gaining valuable experience in communicating psychological concepts to persons who have a different frame of reference.

3. The tradition of medical schools to draw on clinical practitioners for teaching and supervising provides a rich array of different faculty involved in the mental health and medical fields. Since many faculty hold clinical adjunct positions within the school, the students are exposed to a wider variety of different types of practice, background knowledge, and orientations than would be true if all the teaching and supervising were to be done by a core faculty.

4. Location in a medical school provides opportunities for curriculum development in medically related areas such as psychopharmacology, physiology, neurology, and medical information for nonmedical therapists.

The disadvantages of locating in a medical school are probably greater for the faculty than for the students. Some of the more pervasive and perennial difficulties include:

1. Hospital settings and medical schools are very high pressure institutions. Faculty must operate with less time for research, class preparation, and writing than their counterparts in university settings. The impact on quality of teaching is mitigated somewhat by the fact that faculty teach in the areas of their practice and will tend to teach the same courses many times allowing time to develop high-quality instruction. Perhaps a stronger impact is felt by the students who carry full course loads and clinical work, which at times can become an exhausting feat. Similarly, faculty fatigue and burnout is also a concern. However, this model of training has some degree of relevance for clinical work which also tends to be high pressure and allows the students a chance to learn modes of coping which transfer to clinical and professional work later.

2. The disparity between faculty power and remuneration is a subtle, pervasive issue. Nonmedical professionals are reimbursed at a lower level than medical faculty including, of course, psychiatrists. Positions of authority such as department heads, clinic administrators, directorship positions in mental health programs, and so on tend to

be held by those with the M.D. degree with only occasional exceptions. This situation is universal, of course, and not confined to a medical school setting. Psychologists continue to press for parity in the mental health field and in statutory recognition. Until such time as parity is achieved, students will need to learn to separate competency and knowledge from remuneration and power issues in forming a working alliance with the medical profession and a medical school setting is probably as good a place as any to develop clarity on these issues.

In closing this chapter, I would like to make one final comment about the sort of program we have developed at Hahnemann. This model of training could only work in a large, metropolitan teaching hospital. The resources in terms of clinical adjunct faculty and internship settings for about sixty students per year draw on the available resources throughout the entire Philadelphia and suburban area. It is unlikely that a second similar program could be begun in Philadelphia. A wide variety of internship settings must be available that are sufficiently geographically close to the parent institution so that daily commuting is possible. This provides the closely integrated practical and didactic experience which is the cornerstone of our training philosophy. Rural regions or metropolitan areas with few available mental health clinics and institutions or teaching faculty could not develop this type of program.

CHAPTER 10

Development and Operation of a Consortial Model for Professional Education in Clinical Psychology

James H. Johnson, Glenn R. Caddy, David C. Rimm,[1]
Neill Watson, Rashad Saafir, Wallace W. Wilkins,
Ron Giannetti, and Joy Kanarkat
Virginia Consortium for Professional Psychology

In this chapter the architects of the only consortial model program in professional psychology discuss the political and other realities which led to the decision to develop a joint venture program drawing upon the resources of three universities and a medical school. Thereafter, the authors present, in reasonable detail, the guidelines they established in order that the early conflicts and differences of perspective that occurred because of the consortial arrangement did not overpower or disrupt the emergence of this unique endeavor. This chapter also describes the objectives and curriculum of the practitioner-model clinical program of the Virginia consortium. This program and this chapter are considered of particular importance for it would appear likely that in the foreseeable future, universities and other institutional bases which educate professional psychologists will continue to suffer the resource reductions that have plagued higher education in the 1970s. The consortial program described within this chapter offers a model for the future that encourages interinstitution cooperation rather than competition and duplication of effort. As such, the consortial model conserves through distribution the limited resources of each of the institutions which have joined together to foster the education of professional psychologists.

Presently, the only professional program in clinical psychology operating under a consortial model is offered by the Virginia Consortium for Professional Psychology (VCPP). The program was approved by the Virginia State Board of Higher Education in June 1978 and accepted its first class of doctoral students for the fall of that same year. It is anticipated that students in this first class will graduate in July 1982.

143

The VCPP program is offered jointly by four academic departments in four separate institutions: the Department of Psychology of the College of William and Mary (Williamsburg), Norfolk State University (Norfolk), and Old Dominion University (Norfolk), and the Department of Psychiatry and Behavioral Sciences of Eastern Virginia Medical School (Norfolk). The degree is awarded jointly by three of the institutions. (It is anticipated that in the relatively near future Norfolk State University will be elevated to doctoral degree-granting status at which time the name of this institution also will appear on the diploma.)

Background

By 1979, southeastern Virginia was one of the few large metropolitan areas in the United States that was not served by a doctoral training program in clinical psychology. In the early 1970s, representatives from Old Dominion University (ODU) approached the State Council on Higher Education and informally requested that the ODU Department of Psychology be permitted to develop a Ph.D. program in the area of child-clinical psychology. Throughout the late 1960s, the council had been rather permissive in granting approval of new graduate programs. By 1970, however, such permissiveness had provoked criticism from certain legislative quarters and by 1973 the attitude of the council was one of conservatism. The ODU request was denied on the grounds that there were already two operational Ph.D. programs within the state offering training in clinical psychology. The ODU Department of Psychology then began pursuing the possibility of offering the Psy.D. in clinical psychology for it was considered that this program would be far less likely to be construed by the state council as a duplication of ongoing efforts at other state educational institutions. At about the same time, the chairman of the Department of Psychiatry and Behavioral Sciences at Eastern Virginia Medical School (EVMS) also was engaging in preliminary discussions regarding the creation of a Psy.D. program. He had had some administrative involvement in the establishment of the Psy.D. program at Hahnemann Medical College (Philadelphia) and was keenly aware of the unique contribution a Psy.D. training program could provide to the region.

Acute regional needs for high level education in clinical psychology notwithstanding, there was little reason to expect that the state council would approve the development of the two Psy.D. programs in southeastern Virginia. Thus, in late 1973 and early 1974 there was a real sense of competition for the program between these two institutions. In response to these pressures, the idea of a consortial program involving these two institutions as well as the College of William and Mary began to evolve. A consortial arrangement had obvious political advantages. At the time, neither ODU nor EVMS was established enough to have the statewide political connections enjoyed by William and Mary. Thus, for example, if ODU had attempted to "go it alone" the state council might well have denied its proposal—especially with EVMS in an adversary role. On the other hand, given legitimate regional needs for the training of professional psychologists, a consortium including ODU, EVMS, and William and Mary would be in a position to make the state council an offer it would have difficulty in refusing. Thus, in the fall of 1974, the decision was made to approach the council with the idea of a consortial program. The preliminary response on the part of the council was positive, and a planning committee was established under the chairmanship of David Rimm.

By February 1975, the planning committee had completed the program letter of intent. The letter was quickly processed by the faculties and administrations of the respective institutions and submitted to the state council. In 1978, the state council gave formal approval to the letter of intent, and a second committee was charged with preparing the actual program proposal. During the preparation of the proposal, discussions were held with members of the faculty of the Department of Psychology at Norfolk State University (NSU) regarding their participation in the consortial endeavor. As a result of these discussions, NSU became a program participant.

With four institutions participating in the planning process, differences of opinion regarding certain aspects of the program were inevitable. Some of the differences were resolved during the preparation of the letter of intent; others were resolved during the preparation of the program proposal. Representative of the points of controversy were the following:

1. *Rates of tuition.* Some members of the committee argued that no tuition should be charged and that, consistent with Ph.D. training in clinical psychology, when possible, stipends should be awarded to provide support to all students of the program. Others, to the contrary, argued that the Psy.D. is a professional degree. Therefore, relatively high tuition should be charged. A satisfactory compromise was reached wherein students would be charged at a rate equivalent to that charged to law students at William and Mary.
2. *Entrance requirements.* Some members favored relatively stringent formal requirements (e.g., high GPAs and GREs). Others preferred to weigh relevant experience more heavily, pointing to the limited predictive validity of the traditional formal requirements, especially

the GRE. Again, a satisfactory compromise was reached: both formal academic skills and revelant experiences would be considered.

3. *Program governance.* The letter of intent specifically called for a committee of directors, with a rotating chairperson. During the preparation of the program proposal, some committee members questioned the feasibility of such an arrangement, proposing instead that the participating institutions have a single individual as permanent chair. The committee, along with administrators of the participating institutions, discussed the matter. The decision was made to proceed with the original arrangements, at least for the first few years of the program. (In June of 1980, this procedure was changed; see under the heading "Chair of the Council of Directors.")

In June 1978, the state council informed administrative officers of the participating institutions that the program proposal had been approved. The Virginia Consortium for Professional Psychology was a reality.

Program Development

When it became apparent in March 1978 that the program was likely to be approved by the state council, the Consortial Planning Committee began to work in earnest toward the development of an operating program. Because of the consortial nature of the program, there were many more difficulties involved in this developmental effort than would have been experienced had the program resided in a single institution. The questions that confronted the committee were numerous. Given that the courses would be offered at all four schools, where would the records be maintained? Where would applicants apply? How would the students be matriculated, and later graduated? Who would handle student services? Who would collect and disperse fees? Who would approve budgets and disperse funds? How would faculty be appointed? Where would program offices be maintained? Which institutional policies would apply for degree granting? The list goes on and on.

Acknowledging these and many other difficulties associated with the consortial arrangement, the committee decided to first work on establishing a set of rules of procedure for administration of the program. The intent of the committee was to draft a set of procedures that would be ratified by all of the consortial institutions, thereby codifying the operating constraints of the program. These rules were to provide the foundation for the maintenance of the program. To date, they have served their purpose well. As another approach to avoiding possible interinstitutional conflicts, the committee began to publish detailed minutes of each committee meeting and distributed these minutes to relevant administrators and faculty members of each of the consortial institutions, and, after the program began, to the students as well. Therefore, all actions regarding the program are available to all involved persons. If any of these individuals wish to have input regarding decision making, they are free to do so.

Since we began the development of the policies and procedures and the publishing of weekly meeting minutes, there has been a minimum of disagreement among faculty members and administrators.

Program Operation

In this section we will offer the essence of the policies and procedures that were established to structure the operation of the VCPP program. We consider that these operating guidelines may be of considerable value to any other group contemplating a consortial doctoral training program. They indicate a number of problem areas to be addressed and illustrate the method by which these difficulties were managed within the VCPP.

Rules of Operation

The operating rules for the program were approved and endorsed by the Council of Directors (hereafter referred to as the council), and the administrators and departmental faculties of each of the supporting institutions. Ratification proceeded as follows: (a) a majority vote of the council; and (b) a majority vote of the designated administrative officials of the supporting institutions, and a majority vote of each departmental faculty of each supporting institution.

The rules for changing the operating guidelines are the same as those governing the ratification of the operating rules.

Council of Directors

The council is responsible for the administration, development, and implementation of the VCPP program. The council is composed of representatives from each of the supporting institutions, as well as a student representative.

The four institutional representatives are appointed by the academic vice-president of their respective institutions. Each must be centrally involved in the clinical training activities of the supporting institutions. There is an institutional commitment to appoint individuals to the council who are recognized professional role models for faculty, staff, and students. That recognition is earned by state licensure, by formal distinction from professional organizations, such as the status of APA fellow or ABPP diplomate, or by otherwise assuming leadership roles in clinical and/or community psychology.

The student representative is elected by and responsible to the students enrolled in the program.

Each of the five members of the council has one vote in matters of policy. The council meets weekly, or as needed, on a twelve-month basis. A quorum of three institutional representatives, or their designees, is required for a council meeting to be considered official and in session. Specific responsibilities of the council include: (a) conducting weekly meetings and posting minutes of the proceedings, (b) nominating the chair of the council, (c) forming standing committees with specific missions, (d) developing the program's annual budget, (e) recommending student admissions, (f) evaluating student progress, (g) recommending recipients of the Doctor of Psychology degree, (h) evaluating the efficacy of the program in training professional psychologists, (i) assuring that program policies and developments are consistent with the missions and policies of the supporting institutions, (j) assuring that the curriculum meets regional, state, and national requirements for licensure and accreditation, (k) serving as advisors to first-year students, and (l) keeping a portable record system in which duplicates of all correspondence and records will be maintained by the program's secretary.

The council's administrative and reporting situation is unique. While the member institutions are acknowledged as suzerain, the directors and the chairperson are recognized as having a basal commitment and obligation to the program by both the deans and the departmental chairpersons of each of the supporting institutions. This recognition is ratified by the fact that both the directors and the chairperson are provided sufficient release time from their supporting institution to insure the success of the program.

Because federated programs are inherently difficult to maintain and make prosper, it is understood that the primary governing office of the program resides within the council rather than the chairperson, and furthermore, that individual directors speak for the program only when they have the explicit approval of the council as a whole.

Appropriate involvement by the directors is ensured by the chairperson. If at any time there appears to be less than appropriate involvement in the program by any of the directors, it is the chairperson's duty to call this matter to the attention of the council and, through the council, to the designated administrative officials of the relevant supporting institution(s).

All relevant formal communications from the council to the supporting institutions are channeled through the chairperson. These communications are directed to the pertinent official(s) of the respective supporting institutions, with copies to the designated administrative official of that supporting institution.

All formal communications from the supporting institutions to the council concerning administrative matters are through the appropriate administrative official of the supporting institutions (vice-president, graduate dean, registrar, etc.) to the chairperson. In professional matters, all formal communications from a supporting institution are channeled through the appropriate departmental official (department chairperson, department graduate studies committee, department as a whole, etc.) to the chairperson of the council with copies to the designated official of the respective supporting institution. The particular internal mechanisms by which decisions and communications are made within the supporting institutions are left to the faculties of the respective departments of those institutions.

The council chair is appointed for a two-year term by the academic vice-presidents of the supporting institutions. The vice-presidents may consider the nomination(s) of the council, as well as those from other sources. An incumbent chairperson may be nominated and reappointed. In the event that the chair is vacated before the completion of a two-year term, the vice-presidents will appoint a successor for a two-year term from among the available candidates.

Record Keeping and Fiscal Management

A portable record keeping system is maintained among the member institutions. The registrars of each institution have responsibility for the maintenance of this system.

The mechanics for fiscal accounting are administered by ODU. The program budget is developed by the council and forwarded to the vice-presidents of the supporting institutions via the chairperson. The disbursement and accounting of funds within the program is the responsibility of the chairperson.

Standing Committees

Standing committees have been formed to distribute program responsibilities beyond the membership of the council and to ensure that supporting institutions are represented in the specific, task-oriented missions of the committees. Standing committees serve in an advisory capacity to the council. Except for the Student Advisory Committee, membership on standing committees includes at least one representative from each supporting institution, as well as representative(s) from the student body and relevant nonconsortium agencies. Appointments to a standing committee are made jointly by the chair of the council, with the consent of the council, and by the chair of the department with which a committee member is affiliated. Members of the council may serve on standing committees in an ex-officio capacity. Regardless of the actual composition of standing committees, each of the four supporting institutions and the student body are allocated one vote on committee decisions.

Admissions and Financial Aid Committee (AFAC)

This committee develops and maintains procedures for student admissions in accordance with the program admissions policies. Its members review applicants in accordance with those procedures and make recommendations to the council in the form of a rank-ordering of acceptable candidates. The AFAC also recommends levels of financial assistance to be provided to entering and previously matriculated students. That process is to be completed as soon after the application deadline as is feasible, but no later than April 1st.

The AFAC is responsible for specifying the procedures for admissions in public documents describing the program. That committee maintains statistics on the demographic characteristics and qualifications of the applicant pool and of those students admitted, including the geographic area from which applicants were drawn. By February 15 of each year, AFAC submits to the council a report containing information required by the sections on "application," "admission requirements," "student statistics," and "financial aid" of the publication, *Graduate Study in Psychology*. The AFAC also documents compliance of the admissions procedures with guidelines established by the American Psychological Association and other relevant authorities.

Practicum Training Committee (PTC)

This committee serves as the primary mechanism for integrating applied experience with academic training. The PTC is responsible for developing and maintaining guidelines for applied training, for arranging practicum settings each semester, and for serving as liaison between the program and practicum training facilities in the community.

The PTC reviews and evaluates clinical settings for their suitability as practicum training sites in relation to professional standards necessary for training clinical psychologists. The PTC recommends to the council initial and continuing approval of community agencies for providing practicum training. It also works with the applied agencies to increase the quality and quantity of applied training available to program students. Special attention is paid to the quality and intensity of supervision provided by the agency to the training of clinical psychologists.

The PTC maintains an updated roster and vitae of practicum personnel who serve as administrative contacts and as clinical supervisors. That information is available to program students and faculty at each stage of a student's training. That roster also is submitted to the program office by May 15 each year for inclusion in the brochure describing the consortium. Members of the PTC guide the student in the selection of practicum agencies that are most consistent with the educational objectives of the program and the career objectives of the student.

The PTC is responsible for establishing and renewing formal letters-of-agreement between the program and practicum agencies and modifying the program's standard letter-of-agreement to meet the specific requirements of the practicum site. It takes precaution to assure that mutual expectations between supervisor and student are clarified at the outset of the placement and that the expectations of both are met throughout the semester of training. It is the responsibility of the PTC to develop and maintain methods of evaluating the practicum performance of students, as well as the quality of training offered by the practicum agency. Summary evaluations of students, supervisory personnel, and agencies are provided to the chair of the council within 30 days after the completion of each practicum.

Where the practicum agency may provide funding to the student, the PTC is responsible for assuring the council that the student is not exploited as a service provider, but that the student functions as a trainee who, in the course of training, may provide expertise to the agency and to its clientele.

The PTC is responsible for documenting compliance with guidelines established by the American Psychological Association, the Virginia Board of Psychology, and other relevant authorities.

Program Review Committee (PRC)

This committee is responsible for evaluating the efficacy and efficiency of the program in meeting the goals and objectives stated in published descriptions of the program. The PRC develops and maintains procedures for obtaining input on the stucture and functioning of the program from program faculty and students, from practicum supervisors, from administrators of the supporting institutions, and from interested external parties. The PRC documents compliance and recommends changes relevant to guidelines established by the American Psychological Association and other authorities.

The PRC maintains current vitae on program faculty, as well as statistics on the composition of the teaching faculty. Progress reports of committee activities, evaluative findings, and recommendations for corrective action are submitted to the council by June 15, each year.

Comprehensive Examination Committee (CEC)

This committee administers written and oral comprehensive examinations to students, typically at the end of the fifth semester of training, prior to internship. The examination is designed to cover course content as well as clinical competence in a format similar to the state licensing examination.

Student Advisory Committee (SAC)

The Student Advisory Committee is designed to provide student input for the administration and procedures of the program. The SAC is composed of one representative from each class. Each representative is selected by a class in the fall in a manner deemed appropriate by the class. The SAC receives nominations and selects one representative to the council. The SAC also may appoint a student representative to each of the standing committees and ad hoc committees formed by the council. Student representatives have voting privileges on committees on which they serve, except in confidential matters regarding the evaluation of other students.

Admissions

To be considered for admission to the program, an applicant must (a) hold a baccalaureate degree from an accredited institution of higher education; (b) have an acceptable academic background in psychology; (c) present official transcripts indicating coursework completed, grades achieved, degrees received; (d) present official aptitude (verbal, quantitive, analytical), and advanced (psychology) test scores on the Graduate Record Examination; (e) submit a brief statement of approximately 500 words indicating professional goals and academic objectives; and (f) include three letters of recommendation. A personal interview also may be required.

In addition to academic excellence, applicants are reviewed for interest and experience in public sector, social service agencies. Selection efforts are directed particularly to applicants who show a preference to serve the public sector in southeast Virginia. Of equal importance are personal chracteristics conducive to the development of professional competence in dealing effectively with a variety of underserved populations. Academic qualifications of applicants are evaluated to assure that students are capable of meeting the educational requirements of the program.

At present there are no mechanisms for transfer of credits earned at other institutions or for entering the program with advanced standing.

Approximately ten students are admitted to the program each year. After reviewing all applicants, the Admissions and Financial Aid Committee submits recommendations to the council, which recommends to the graduate deans. After reviewing candidates' records, the graduate dean designated by the graduate deans of the supporting institutions admits students to the program on behalf of the supporting institutions. That review process assures that the candidates present credentials that are consistent with program goals and that meet standards for doctoral training established by the State Council of Higher Education for Virginia.

Curriculum

The primary goal of the curriculum is to provide students with a very high level of professionally-oriented training. The curriculum involves a sequence of courses designed to ensure the mastery of the knowledge and skills necessary for professional competence. Courses provide students with a foundation in relevant areas of the science of psychology, with clinically-related didactic instruction, and with applied experiences in the delivery and evaluation of services.

In the first, second, and fourth years of training, students engage in a full-time sequence of academic and practicum courses during fall, spring, and summer sessions. A full-time clinical internship is taken during the third year of training.

The curriculum should include coursework in the following areas of psychological science that are relevant to professional practice: (a) life span psychology; (b) social psychology; (c) physiological psychology and perception; (d) learning, cognition, and motivation; (e) personality; (f) statistics; (g) research design; (h) history and systems in psychology.

In the first two years, coursework should also include the following topics as foundations in the professional practice: (a) introduction to professional psychology (overview, including ethics), (b) community psychology, (c) group dynamics, (d) psychopathology, (e) therapeutic relationships and interviewing techniques, (f) practica, (g) professional growth, (h) assessment, (i) program evaluation, (j) childhood disorders, (k) intercultural psychology, (l) social systems and intervention, (m) marriage and family, (n) therapeutic interventions (behavioral, bio-medical, humanistic-existential, psychodynamic), (o) professional growth, and (p) topic modules such as human sexuality, gerontology, addiction, rural and urban problems, vocational, crisis interventions, forensic psychology, sexism, racism, poverty, school-related problems, social change, and prevention.

In the fourth year, electives and practica are coordinated with the dissertation in order to constitute an area of specialization. In addition, coursework inlcudes: (a) technology in mental health care, (b) administration (service delivery, grantsmanship, etc.), (c) behavioral medicine.

The curriculum published in the program catalog at the time a student matriculates is the set of courses required by the program. Although at present there are no mechanisms for transferring credits earned at other institutions, a student may be exempted from taking a required course if the student can demonstrate mastery of the course content, through a written or oral examination, to the satisfaction of the course instructor and the council. Exemption from a required course does not reduce the total number of credits required of a student. Exemption allows the student to substitute an elective course of equal credit in place of the exempted course. The student is responsible for timely application to the council for the proficiency examination. The entire exemption process must be completed no later than one week after the beginning of the course in question.

Graduate Student Support Systems

Advising. Entering students are assigned a faculty advisor from among the members of the council. Second-year students select their own advisors from faculty at large, and register their advisor with the program secretary by the end of the fourth semester. Students are encouraged to select an advisor whose interests are consonant with their own and who may eventually serve to guide and direct the student's dissertation.

Financial Aid. At present, three of the supporting institutions, EVMS, ODU, and William and Mary contribute to fellowship support administered through the program. Students who are making normal progress and who are in good standing in the program may compete for those sources of support. Applications for program support are submitted to the chair of the Admissions and Financial Aid Committee for consideration and award.

Independent of support administered through the program, students may compete for financial support administered through the School of Graduate Studies at ODU. Information and application forms may be obtained from the ODU School of Graduate Studies and are to be returned to the ODU representative to the council who nominates the student for consideration by the ODU dean of graduate studies.

Practicum Placement. Through the Practicum Training Committee, students are placed in community agencies in a manner to maximize the training benefits to the students and the contributions of the student to the agency. Prior to placement, the Practicum Training Committee arranges for letters of agreement between the practicum agency and the program to clarify general expectations for both parties. At the time of placement, the student is responsible for initiating a specific contract describing the nature of the training experience to be obtained during the semester of placement. Toward the end of the placement, students also are responsible for initiating a mutual evaluation process between the student and the agency supervisor. Forms for the contract, for the students' evaluation of the agency, and for the agency supervisors' evaluation of the students can be obtained from the chair of the Practicum Training Committee. They are to be returned to the faculty member responsible for administering the practicum course during the particular semester.

Institutional Privileges. Graduate students enrolled in the program are considered to be enrolled full-time in all four supporting institutions and have access to the same privileges as any other full-time student enrolled in the institutions. Among those privileges are access to the computing centers, libraries, bookstores, on-campus parking, student discounts to athletic events, health insurance, and student health services.

Travel. To reduce the financial burden to the student, the program provides state vehicles for commuting to classes at the different institutions. Car pools involving state vehicles are formed at ODU and William and Mary.

Comprehensive Examination

In the spring semester of the second year there is an evaluation of each student by means of written and oral comprehensive examinations that cover course content and clinical competence. The philosophy of the examinations is to sample a broad range of knowledge in the field of psychology as well as to focus on the area of clinical practice. The examination is patterned after the format of typical state licensing examinations. The Comprehensive Examination Committee is responsible for the construction and scoring of all sections of the examination.

The exam is given during a two-day period. The first day is devoted to two written sections. The three-hour, multiple-choice section is given in the morning and the four-hour essay section is given in the afternoon of the first day. The second day involves individual, one-hour oral examinations for each student.

The multiple-choice section is modeled after the national AASPB examination. Individual multiple-choice items will be pooled from professors of courses taken by the class of examinees. This section will encompass a wide range of subjects from general psychology.

The essay section will emphasize theoretical and practical clinical material. The essay format allows examinees to choose to answer a limited number of questions from among the several questions presented. There will be one required question that will address ethical and legal standards for practicing psychologists. All examinations are scored on a pass/fail basis after having been reviewed by at least two different evaluators. Students will be notified of the results as soon as possible after the examination.

For the oral section of the comprehensive examination, students submit a work sample to the examination committee as evidence of their clinical proficiency. That work sample consists of an evaluative assessment report and a therapy case study, including a tape recording and written transcript of a therapy session. In addition, students are to answer questions on clinical and professional issues.

Students must pass all three sections of the comprehensive examination before entering candidacy and before beginning coursework in the fourth year of training. Students who fail any sections of the comprehensive examination must retake those sections when the examination is administered the following year.

Academic Standing

Students' records are reviewed at the end of each semester. A student is considered to be *in good academic standing* if a cumulative GPA of 3.00 on a 4.00 scale is maintained while making normal progress through the required sequence of coursework.

A student is placed on academic *probation* if the cumulative GPA is below 3.00 at the end of any semester. A student may be on academic probation for a maximum of two semesters.

A student may be *suspended indefinitely* upon recommendation by the council to the graduate deans of the supporting institutions (a) for failure to increase the cumulative GPA to 3.00 within two semesters after having been placed on academic probation, (b) for failure to pass all sections of the comprehensive examination before beginning the fourth year of training, or (c) for failure to adhere to the ethical principles of the American Psychological Association. A student who is suspended indefinitely is no longer in good academic standing and is not authorized to take graduate courses which later could be transferred for credit within the program. Upon written appeal by the student, the council may reconsider the appellant's case. Recommendation to remove suspension will be made to the graduate deans of the supporting institutions, if there is sufficient evidence predictive of the appellant's future success in the program.

A student who wishes to withdraw temporarily from the program must submit, through his/her advisor, a written request for a hearing with the council. The request will outline the reasons for withdrawing. The council will approve or deny the request. An approved request will specify the maximum period of time that the student may be absent from the program.

Unless special circumstances exist, the maximum period of time will be no more than one calendar year. At the end of the approved absence, a student may apply for an extension by requesting another hearing. A student who is absent from the program without the approval of the council will be terminated from the program.

A student returning from an approved absence will be reinstated upon request to the council and commence study in the first semester following the request. However, the council cannot guarantee that the specific courses required by the student will be offered that semester. A student who was in good standing at the time of withdrawal will be in good standing upon returning to the program.

The council will make a reasonable effort to notify students of their academic status. Ultimately, however, it is the responsibility of each student to consult with the council to determine his/her academic status.

Candidacy

Admission. A student will be admitted to candidacy for the degree of Doctor of Psychology upon recommendation of the council to the graduate deans and after the student has: (1) passed all sections of the comprehensive examination, (2) completed at least the first two years of the program curriculum, (3) successfully completed the internship requirement, (4) obtained approval for the dissertation proposal from his/her dissertation committee, and (5) filed the approved dissertation proposal with the graduate dean of the supporting institutions. Those experiences culminate with the dissertation and its defense.

Dissertation Committee. The function of the dissertation committee is to direct and supervise dissertation research. The dissertation committee is composed of at least three members, who are drawn from the full-time faculties of at least two of the supporting institutions. The director of the dissertation research must be knowledgeable in the field of specialization of the proposed dissertation, and must have the approval of the graduate deans, or their designates. Membership of the dissertation committee may also be extended to a nonconsortium person with special knowledge of the dissertation topic area. Voting privileges can be provided to such specialists upon the recommendation of the dissertation director and the approval of the Graduate Dean. The graduate deans of the supporting institutions are *ex officio* members of all dissertation committees.

The director of the dissertation committee serves as the chair of the dissertation committee and as the moderator of the dissertation defense, ruling on questions of procedure and protocol that may arise during the defense. The chair represents the graduate deans, to all of whom that individual makes a complete and prompt report of the defense. The dissertation and its defense must have the majority approval of the dissertation committee. When the defense is successfully completed, the original and four copies of the dissertation are submitted along with the committee's recommendation to the graduate dean designated by the graduate deans of the supporting institutions for binding and distribution to the Program Office and the supporting institutions. In case of failure, the dissertation committee may recommend that the candidate be terminated from the program, or be reexamined no earlier than three months after the first examination. General regulations and procedures governing the submission of a doctoral dissertation are given in the *Guide for Preparation of Theses and Dissertations,* available at ODU.

At least two weeks prior to the defense, the time and place of the oral examination must be filed with the graduate deans of the supporting institutions. That information is published in the appropriate university news media. All interested members of the university communities are encouraged to attend the examination.

Graduation

The general requirements of the Doctor of Psychology degree are provided in the catalogs of the degree-granting institutions.

To be awarded the degree of Doctor of Psychology, the student must have met the following specific requirements which shall also be published in the program catalog:

1. The successful completion of three full years (fall, spring, and summer semesters) of full-time study beyond the baccalaureate, or the equivalent, is required. In addition, the successful completion of an internship that is a full-time experience for one calendar year, or a half-time experience for two calendar years, with at least two hours per week of formally scheduled individual supervision, is required.
2. At least 6 semesters and 72 semester hours shall be in residence in the program, with the student being registered in the program during the semester in which the degree requirements are completed.
3. Each doctoral student must pass the comprehensive written and oral qualifying examination before being admitted to candidacy.
4. Each student must propose, conduct, and successfully defend a clinical dissertation with a strong evaluative component in the student's area of specialization. The candidate is expected to show a mastery of the area of specialization within which the dissertation was conducted.
5. Students are required to have a GPA of 3.00 or better to be awarded the Psy.D. degree. Those who complete the course requirements for the degree but have deficiency in GPA may be given an opportunity to increase their GPA by repeating up to nine credits of prior coursework in which relative deficiencies were exhibited.
6. All requirements for the doctoral degree must be completed within seven (7) calendar years from the time the student is admitted to the doctoral program.

Formal application for the degree must be filed with the graduate deans no later than 90 days prior to the end of the semester, or 60 days prior to the end of the summer semester, in which the student expects to complete the requirements for graduation.

Conclusion

These operating guidelines were developed because it was recognized from the outset that unless a set of rules of procedure were developed for the VCPP program, and unless these rules were supported by each of the member institutions, the program would have little chance of surviving. The methods for resolving problems that emerge whenever a number of separate agencies, each with slightly differing ideologies and political identities, set off down a cooperative path had to be planned for in order that the program could maximize the prospects for its success. The operating procedures that were developed during the planning and early implementation phases of the VCPP program are unique. Yet, these rules have both facilitated the development and helped the structure of this cooperative venture.

At the beginning of the third year of operation, this first and still only consortial model program is faring particularly well. There are now 29 students in the program and all eight students of the first class have obtained internship placements. Students have been drawn to the program from geographical areas ranging from Texas to Massachusetts. Administration and coursework follows a truly consortial model. Weekly meetings of the council are rotated from institution to institution; faculty assigned to teach courses within the program are paid by their respective institutions, and the basic program budget is contributed to by each of the supporting institutions.

The VCPP has become a reality despite the many obstacles that faced its development and early operation. It is organized in a way that may seem cumbersome to many, but this organization results from the needs of the situation. Difficult as it has been to develop, the success of the VCPP supports the notion that a consortial model for professional training in clinical psychology can flourish.

Notes

1. Dr. Rimm left Old Dominion University prior to the commencement of the Virginia consortium program. Nevertheless, his contribution to the early development of the consortial model was major and deserves special recognition.
2. Dr. Wilkins drafted much of the current policies and procedures for the Virginia consortium from an earlier draft developed by the other authors.

PART D
Conclusion

CHAPTER 11

Issues and Resolutions of the Virginia Beach Conference and Current Developments

Neill Watson
Virginia Consortium for Professional Psychology

In this concluding chapter, the resolutions adopted by the Virginia Beach conferees are discussed in the context of the issues from which the resolutions evolved. Dr. Watson's commentary on each of the resolutions also addressed briefly the developments in these issues since the time of the conference in an effort to clarify problems to be solved within professional psychology and within psychology as a whole.

The events of the decade before the conference at Virginia Beach provide an historical context for understanding the issues that were of concern to the conference. In the late 1960s, as Peterson describes in detail in his chapter, a large movement within professional psychology and a smaller movement within academic departments of psychology began to establish programs based on a new model for the education of practitioners. Many new programs in professional psychology developed at an accelerating pace, especially after the Vail conference endorsed the concept of the practitioner-model of education in 1973 (Korman, 1976). The National Council of Schools of Professional Psychology was organized in 1976 and had 25 members as of 1978. By the end of 1978 there were 30 practitioner-model programs instead of the four programs that were in existence a decade before.

Of the new programs, a large number had not been in existence long enough to be accredited by the APA, and some were not in regionally accredited educational institutions (see Table 1.2). The awareness that large numbers of professional psychologists were being educated in programs of unknown quality resulted in the concern within the professional psychology community that many inadequately trained practitioners might be produced. For example, the appearance of several independent schools of professional psychology in California caused psychologists in that state to communicate their concern to the APA about whether these programs met professional standards (Polonsky, Fox, Wiens, Dixon, Freedman, & Shapiro, 1979).

There was clearly a need for communication among the practitioner-model programs about how best to educate professional psychologists. Though the Vail conference had endorsed the concept of a practitioner model, the specifics of the model had not yet been developed. The conference at Virginia Beach, which included the directors or representatives of many of the practitioner-model programs in existence and in the planning stages, provided a forum for communication about current practices and for deliberation about the development of standards in the education of professional psychologists.

The conference considered a number of issues in the education of professional psychologists. In his chapter, Peterson identifies several questions that were the subject of discussion and debate: How do we gauge the public need for psychological services? How should we select students for careers in professional psychology? How do we evaluate professional competence in psychology? What should we teach professional psychologists? Who should teach professional psychologists? How do we evaluate educational programs in professional psychology? What organizations are most effective for training professional psychologists? The conference also considered the accreditation criteria for programs in professional psychology that were in the process of being revised by the APA (APA Task Force, 1978).

After addressing these issues in papers and discussions, the conferees adopted resolutions concerned with the need for an increase in the number of professional psychologists, the selection and evaluation of students, the curricula of practitioner-model programs, the administrative structures of the programs, and criteria for the accreditation of programs. The resolutions were drafted by a committee of the conference that consisted of Glenn R. Caddy, Gordon Derner, Ronald E. Fox, James H. Johnson, Arthur L. Kovacs, and Donald R. Peterson.

The resolutions of the conference are presented below. Included with each resolution is commentary on the issues addressed and commentary on developments since the time of the conference.

Resolutions

Resolution 1. It has been well documented that there exists a serious undersupply of professional psychologists available to serve the mental health needs of the American public (e.g., Gottfredson & Dyer, 1978; Wellner & Mills, note 1, later published as Mills, Wellner, & VandenBos, 1979). In addition to traditional mental health careers, other career opportunities already exist and continue to develop for professional psychologists to provide services for normative life crises, for the psychological correlates of health problems, for crime and delinquency, and for other psychosocial problems. Despite these obvious needs, each year large numbers of well-qualified applicants for graduate study in professional psychology are denied opportunity for training. It is strongly in the public interest that psychology markedly increase opportunities for doctoral education in professional psychology.

Whether there is a manpower shortage in mental health is a question that is currently being reevaluated. The documentation of a shortage cited in the first resolution refers to reports that estimate the number of doctoral level psychologists who provide services on a part-time or full-time basis to be between 15,000 and 18,500 (Gottfredson & Dyer, 1978; Mills, Wellner, & VandenBos, 1979). In comparison to the estimate that 15 percent of the American population, or 34 million individuals, are in need of some type of mental health service (U.S. President's Commission on Mental Health, 1978), the number of professional psychologists appear to be inadequate. However, the assessment of the need for services is a complex problem (Liptzin, 1978), and estimates have varied from 1 percent to 60 percent on the criteria of need employed (Dohrenwend & Dohrenwend, 1974).

Since the time of the conference, several reports have addressed the issue of manpower requirements in mental health. VandenBos, Nelson, Stapp, Olmedo, Coates, & Batchelor (note 2) estimate the current shortage of between 12,000 and 20,000 professional psychologists. Utilizing more conservative criteria of need, Liptzin (1978) estimates a shortage of about 8,500 professional psychologists by 1981. On the supply side of a supply/demand analysis, Richards (note 3) estimates that there are presently between 10,000 and 13,000 doctoral students enrolled in clinical psychology,[1] and he concludes that the current number of students appears to meet or exceed the manpower requirement estimated by VandenBos et al. (note 2). Contrary to the first resolution, these reports indicate that there may be no need for an increase in educational opportunities in professional psychology. However, because of the disparities among the various estimates of need, it seems that close attention should be given to monitoring manpower requirements.

Though there may be little or no need for an increase in the total number of professional psychologists, there is evidence of a problem in the distribution of this resource. It is estimated that over half of the available psychological services are provided in private practice (Gottfredson & Dyer, 1978), and that practitioners are concentrated in affluent urban areas (Richards & Gottfredson, 1978). A particular need for more services to the elderly, children, minorities, and rural populations, as well as a need for preventive services, has been identified (U.S. President's Commission on Mental Health, 1978; VandenBos et al., note 2). The major issue in regard to manpower requirements, then, is that there should be a coordination between identified social needs and the education of professional psychologists.

In view of the problem of a maldistribution of professional psychologists, there arises the question of how well professional training programs will meet the needs for mental health care that are not being met by the present service delivery system. Will professional programs take these needs into account in selecting and educating practitioners? The relatively high rate of compensation in the private sector, which will probably provide employment for an influx of practitioners for a significant period of time, makes it likely that large numbers of prospective students will choose the career goal of private practice. The training of private practitioners, however, probably would result in the delivery of services to only a limited segment of the population. The services available in the private sector may be limited to the most lucrative services, i.e., the individual and group remediation approaches most appropriate to middle and upper socioeconomic populations. There appear to be no incentives in the private sector that would encourage the development and delivery of services that are needed by presently underserved populations.

It is the author's position that training programs in professional psychology have a responsibility to consider the unmet needs in the mental health care systems in the selection and education of professional psychologists. If mainly private practitioners are produced, then the mental health needs of large segments of our society may go unmet. It is probably only in the public sector that services to underserved populations, especially preventive services, will be developed and delivered. However, if these mental health needs are to be met, it will require more than a commitment by training programs in professional psychology. The contingencies in the public sector must be reorganized to encourage professional psychologists, as well as other mental health practitioners, to enter the public sector rather than the private sector. Salaries should be increased to attract the best practitioners. Training should be supported by public funds with the requirement that the recipient practice in the public sector for a specified number of years. Moreover, state laws should require that psychologists in public service be licensed, in order to ensure the quality of services in the public sector.

At least three of the current practitioner-model programs in professional psychology are concerned expressly with the problem of the maldistribution of professional psychologists. The California School of Professional Psychology has a program on its Fresno campus that prepares students for service delivery in rural areas. The programs of the Hahnemann Medical College and of the Virginia Consortium for Professional Psychology emphasize training in public sector mental health care for currently underserved segments of the population. Such programs are examples of the much needed coordination of the training of practitioners with the areas that have the greatest need for psychological services.

Preventive services are lacking in the mental health care delivery system. Recognizing this fact, the United States President's Commission on Mental Health (1978) has recommended major new federally supported efforts to prevent psychological disorders. Albee (1959, 1968), identifying a manpower shortage in mental health, has argued that the solution is primary prevention. In his view, adequate numbers of professionals to provide remedial services cannot be trained in the foreseeable future. Even if the number of professionals can be increased to a level commensurate with the need for remedial services, it would not be the humane solution to work to alleviate suffering when it is possible to work to prevent suffering.

In the author's view, the mandate for the training of professional psychologists is clear: programs in professional psychology should give priority to educating practitioners in methods of prevention. The conceptual paradigm and intervention strategies that are being developed in community psychology promise to provide the necessary tools for prevention. Whether professional programs will move in the direction of prevention is an important issue. Albee (1979) has argued that, from the point of view of psychologists trained in remediation, prevention is bad for business, and that as a result there is presently resistance on the part of mental health professionals to the recommendations for preventive efforts made by the president's commission. An emphasis on prevention eventually will decrease the need for professional psychologists and limit the growth of programs in professional psychology. There is an important question of whether professional programs will be selfless enough to place an emphasis on preventive methods.

The present undersupply of professional psychologists indicates the importance of increasing the number of doctoral programs that educate practitioners. The demand on the part of students for professional training is extremely high, and each year many qualified applicants are rejected by existing programs. Nyman (1973) has reported that the ratio of acceptances to rejections in clinical psychology, corrected for multiple applications, was 4.6, whereas the ratio for medical school candidates was only 2.7. It appears that the availability of applicants well may encourage the development of new programs in professional psychology. However, as Peterson recommends in his chapter, the increase in educational opportunities in professional psychology should proceed at a moderate rate, and the need for professional psychologists should be monitored in order to avoid an oversupply. Moreover, the major issue in regard to manpower is that there should be a coordination of training with identified social needs together with a special emphasis on prevention.

> *Resolution 2.* Criteria for admissions to professional programs should give adequate attention to both inter- and intrapersonal attributes of applicants, as well as to standard achievement measures. Traditionally, selection procedures have heavily weighted grades and scores on standard tests and measures. There is reason to doubt that these criteria are effective predictors of success in professional psychology. Large scale research studies are urgently needed to develop criteria with demonstrated relevance to professional functioning. Professional programs need to collaborate in evaluating themselves and in searching for relevant predictors.

The second resolution addresses several interrelated issues concerning the need for research to evaluate the effectiveness of current practices in the education of professional psychologists. The central issue is the need for valid measures of professional competence. Research on the effectiveness of the educational programs and research concerned with the identification of valid admissions criteria depend on measures of professional competence and other outcome criteria yet to be developed.

As the survey reported in Shannon's chapter indicates, admissions committees in practitioner-model programs still rely heavily on grade-point averages and achievement test scores. These criteria typically are used to reduce the pool of applicants to a small number, and then non-academic criteria are taken into consideration. There is no research to indicate whether this method, or any other method, succeeds in identifying the best candidates for training in professional psychology. An important aspect of the second resolution is its mandate that professional programs collaborate in research to identify the criteria that predict the attainment of professional competence.

A prerequisite for research on predictors of professional competence is the development of valid methods for the assessment of professional competence. Peterson's comment was well taken when he expressed his concern regarding how little has been done toward measuring the competence of its practitioners by a profession that is presumed to be expert in the assessment of human behavior. The reasons for immediate attention to the design of methods for measuring competence are manifold. These methods are needed, not only for research to determine revelant admissions criteria, but also for the evaluation of students and of the effectiveness of professional psychology training programs themselves. In this regard, the second resolution states that programs should collaborate in evaluating themselves.

> *Resolution 3.* The curriculum in professional psychology must ensure the mastery of a comprehensive, empirically-based body of knowledge and skills in psychology in an orderly, sequential fashion designated to meet accepted standards of professional competence (APA, 1977). The program must create a sense of professional identity and responsibility for client welfare, including a commitment to the ongoing evaluation of the efficiency and effectiveness of services. In order to do so, the training program must provide extensive, carefully supervised practice in professional psychology by qualified psychological practitioners beginning in the first year of training.

This third resolution provides guidelines for the curricula of practitioner-model programs. In program evaluation terms, the resolution provides broad quality assurance guidelines for the education of practitioners. However, there is no evidence for the effectiveness of the recommended curriculum in producing competent professionals. The effectiveness of curricula based on the practitioner-model, and of curricula based on the scientist-practitioner model, should be evaluated in research on the outcomes of the various educational programs.

The resolution states that the practitioner must be trained comprehensively in the knowledge and skills that are based on empirical research. This aspect of the resolution recognizes, as did one of the resolutions of the Vail conference (Korman, 1976), that psychological knowledge that forms the foundation necessary for professional practice. Though the curricula of practitioner-model programs are not designed to train students to carry out basic research, students should be provided with skills to evaluate the validity of basic research so that they can be critical consumers of future empirical findings.

An essential point of the resolution is that curricula must include extensive practicum training from the beginning of the program. The development of professional skills is to be emphasized throughout the course of study and not relegated mainly to the internship year, as has been common in the scientific-practitioner programs. Professional skills are to be taught by qualified psychological practitioners who serve as role models as well as provide intensive supervision. The emphasis on applied training by practicing psychologists is intended to impart to the student a strong professional identity as a service provider responsible for client welfare. The concern in the resolution with the creation of an identity as a professional psychologist stems from observations, such as that made by Fishman in his chapter, that the scientist-practitioner-model programs have been in academic cultures that typically have not held and transmitted the values of service delivery. The curricula of practitioner-model programs must transmit the values and skills necessary for meeting the accepted standards of professional competence as defined in the *Standards for Providers of Psychological Services* (APA, 1977).

One of the standards for service providers is that "there shall be periodic, systematic, and effective evaluations of psychological services" (APA, 1977, p. 10). The resolution stresses the commitment to the continual evaluation of the efficiency and effectiveness of services. To meet this standard, programs must provide thorough training in evaluative research. Thus, the basic research orientation of the scientist-practitioner-model programs is to be replaced by an applied research orientation in practitioner-model programs. Expertise in evaluative research is essential for accountability within the profession and for accountability to the sources of funding and to the users of services. The importance of training in program evaluation is also endorsed by Fox and Rodgers in their principles for curriculum development and by Fishman in his discussion of practicum training in practitioner-model programs. However, an examination of the curricula of the existing practitioner-model programs reveals that only a small percentage of the programs emphasize evaluative research.

The curricula of the practitioner-model programs already in operation typically provide training in a comprehensive set of professional competencies that range from the biopsychological level to the social system level of understanding human behavior. Students learn assessement and intervention with the individual, the small group, the family, the organization, and the community. With the opportunity to develop these skills from the beginning of the curriculum, students in practitioner-model programs are prepared to utilize the year of internship for learning at a more advanced stage than has been typical for the student in the scientist-practitioner-model programs.

In their chapter on curriculum, Fox and Rodgers consider the best settings for applied clinical training to be centers for psychological services administered by the educational programs themselves. The importance of the development of psychological service centers of this type was emphasized by Albee at the Chicago conference (Hoch, Ross, & Winder, 1966). It will be interesting to see whether such facilities will be developed and whether they will have a beneficial impact on clinical training as well as service delivery.

> *Resolution 4.* Training in professional psychology, as described in the preceding resolutions, can be provided best in university-based schools of professional psychology. Under special conditions, this training may be provided in freestanding professional schools if these are sensitive to the maintenance of a suitable scholarly orientation. University psychology departments also have provided quality professional education when the departmental faculty and the administration have been committed to the special demands of such education. Proprietary institutions and external degree programs may have special problems in maintaining standards of scholarship and professional training. Proprietary schools and external degree programs bear a special responsibility in demonstrating that they are capable of providing quality education.

The concern about the organizational structure of programs in professional psychology stems from the quality assurance issue of whether each program has adequate academic and clinical resources to educate competent practitioners. The issue of adequate resources also has been raised by psychologists concerned about the appearance of a number of independent schools in their state (Polonsky et al., 1979) and by the Council of Graduate Departments of Psychology, which recently adopted a resolution stating that the development of programs in professional psychology be restricted to regionally accredited colleges and universities (Meyer, note 4).

The fourth resolution states that the type of educational setting best suited for the training of psychological practitioners is a professional school within a university. The importance of the university setting is that it is considered to be a milieu that will ensure the maintenance of high standards of educational excellence. There is concern that independent professional schools may not exercise the quality control that would be required of a university professional school by the larger institution of which it is a part. A further concern is that independent professional schools may not have the libraries and other resources necessary for academic excellence. However, the resolution acknowledges that independent schools can provide quality education if they take steps to satisfy the requirements for academic standards and resources.

Psychology departments of universities are recognized in the resolution as able to provide quality professional education if they have a commitment to the training of practitioners. However, the primary commitment of clinical programs in departments of psychology typically has been to the training of researchers, and these programs often have looked with disfavor upon careers in clinical practice. For example, the fact that a large number of their graduates were becoming practitioners, rather than researchers, contributed significantly to the decisions of Harvard University and Stanford University to terminate their programs in clinical psychology. Only a few psychology departments have had clinical programs that valued the training of practitioners. The resolution recognizes that these departments have provided quality professional education. Since the commitment to the training of practitioners has been rare in departments of psychology, the resolution considers a professional school within a university a better setting for such training.

Two types of organizations, proprietary schools and external degree programs, are considered in the resolution to have major drawbacks that may make them unsuitable settings for the education of professional psychologists. In the case of proprietary schools, the need to generate a profit may result in hiring large numbers of part-time faculty and in admitting many more students than can be trained as intensively as is necessary for the development of professional competence. In external degree programs, it may not be possible to exercise sufficient control over the students' training to ensure an educational experience of high quality. The resolution states that these types of organizations have a special responsibility to demonstrate their effectiveness.

Though university-based professional schools are considered in the fourth resolution to be the most capable of providing quality education, there is no evidence for the differential effectiveness of the various organizational settings in educating competent practitioners. As stated in debate at the conference, this is an issue to be resolved through evaluative research.

> *Resolution 5.* The standards of accreditation for professional psychology programs should include, in addition to generic standards, specific standards for the several professional specialties. However, these specialty standards should not be developed in a manner that may interfere with the right of university departments to set academic standards in psychology for programs that are not directed toward professional practice.

At the time of the conference at Virginia Beach, the APA was revising its accreditation criteria for programs in professional psychology (APA Task Force, 1978). In response to the draft of generic criteria in circulation at the time, the fifth resolution advocated the inclusion of criteria specific to each area of professional specialization, i.e., clinical, counseling, school, and industrial-organizational psychology. However, the criteria that were finally adopted by the APA remained only generic in nature (APA, 1979). Also, only generic criteria are currently being considered by the APA Task Force on Education and Credentialing (Arnold, note 5), which is developing criteria for the designation of programs in professional psychology by the proposed National Commission on Education and Credentialing (Wellner, note 6). Though specific criteria, in the opinion of the conferees, can provide more rigorous quality control than generic criteria, specific criteria can be based at present only on "best guesses" until evaluative research provides data-based guidelines.

The second major point in the resolution is that the criteria for the accreditation of professional programs should not affect programs in academic psychology that train basic scientists. In order to determine which programs are to be judged by the accreditation criteria for professional training, a clear distinction must be made between professional programs and research programs. The recently adopted accreditation criteria (APA, 1979) provide a mechanism for making such a distinction in that they require a program seeking accreditation to have declared explicitly and publicly the mission of the program.

The present accreditation criteria (APA, 1979) consider both the scientist-practitioner model and the practitioner model as appropriate for the training of psychologists to deliver mental health services. At the conference, many considered the distinction between the two models to be critical, with the scientist-practitioner model being more appropriate for the training of psychologists for basic research and the practitioner model being more appropriate for the training of psychologists for service delivery. A similar distinction had been made at the Vail conference in 1973 (Korman, 1976).

> *Resolution 6.* Professional psychology training programs must demonstrate a commitment to excellence. Standards of excellence for professional programs will differ in some respects from those of research programs. It is essential, however, that training in professional psychology be as rigorous and demanding as that associated with traditional research-oriented programs. The doctorate in professional psychology must not be, or be seen to be, inferior to the research-oriented training program.

The sixth resolution, a commitment to excellence in the education of professional psychologists, is a statement of the intent of the foregoing resolutions. Programs that train practitioners have objectives and standards that necessarily differ in nature from the objectives and standards of programs that train researchers. Different criteria should be used in the selection of students, in the design of the curriculum, and in the evaluation of professional competence. However, professional programs should not differ from research programs in terms of the rigor of the standards. Programs based on the practitioner model must educate professionals in the type of problem-solving skills considered by Korchin (1976) to epitomize the goals of doctoral education in both scientific and professional psychology.

An Unresolved Issue

An issue of debate at the conference was whether the Psy.D. or the Ph.D. degree should be awarded in programs based on the practitioner-model. Somewhat less than half of the recently established practitioner-model programs award the Psy.D.; however, the California School of Professional Psychology, the Institute of Advanced Psychological Studies at Adelphia University, and many others award the Ph.D. In the debate, it was argued by some that the Ph.D. is the preferable degree because it has a long history as the doctorate of highest academic achievement. The established standards for programs that award the Ph.D. would ensure that practitioner-model programs would be of the highest quality. On the other side of the debate, it was argued that the Ph.D., as the established credential of the scholar, is inappropriate as a certificate of professional competence for the practitioner. More importantly, the requirements that may be imposed on programs that choose to award the Ph.D. may, in many universities, have an undesirable impact on the content of the educational program. As a new degree, the Psy.D. can be tied to standards developed specifically for the training of professional psychologists. There would be no doubt about the purpose or content of programs that award the Psy.D.; the training would be unambiguously directed toward the delivery of psychological services.

Why have only one degree for the certification of professional competence? One reason is that there is the potential for a two-tiered, divisive system within professional psychology, with the Ph.D. considered the superior degree. Another reason is that one degree would make it easier to enforce quality control over professional training at a number of different levels of governance. Another compelling reason is that two degrees may confuse the public.

At the Vail conference (Korman, 1976) it was recommended that the Psy.D. be awarded by practitioner-model programs and that the Ph.D.

be awarded by scientist-practitioner-model programs. In the accreditation criteria of the APA (APA, 1979), however, the Ph.D. is considered appropriate for scientist-practitioner-model programs, and either the Ph.D. or Psy.D. is considered appropriate for practitioner-model programs. It seems apparent, at least at the present time, that programs in professional psychology are not being identified by their own unique degree. However, it is interesting to note that a large proportion of the most recently developed practitioner-model programs in professional psychology do award the Psy.D. degree (see Table 1.2).

Questions for the Future

What effects will the emergence of the new practitioner-model programs in professional psychology have on the older programs that are based on the scientist-practitioner model? The answer to this question will probably vary for different programs. One possibility is that some of the scientist-practitioner-model programs may more clearly define themselves as providing research training. Programs with a commitment to scientific training may be more likely to attract students who have research interests, since the students with clinical interests have an alternative not previously available. For example, Peterson said at the conference that the Ph.D. program in clinical psychology at Rutgers became more focused on research when Rutgers established a Psy.D. program in clinical psychology. Another possibility is that some of the scientist-practitioner-model programs may define themselves as providing training for practitioners. Many of these programs probably would have to make significant changes in their curricula in order to meet the revised APA accreditation guidelines for professional programs (APA, 1979). The curriculum changes would likely be even greater if the programs choose to provide the level of practicum training characteristic of the Psy.D. programs. Overall, the emergence of explicitly professional programs may cause a major reevaluation of educational objectives within the scientist-practitioner-model programs and result in a choice between the objectives of research and practice.

With a greater distinction between education for basic research and education for practice, what are the implications for the relationship between research and practice? How can psychology as a whole assure the mutual accountability of research and practice? It is important to consider that many practitioner-model programs provide training toward the objectives that their students be competent consumers of basic research and evaluators of psychological services. The degree to which research and practice will have a mutually beneficial relationship depends, in part, on how well practitioner-model programs achieve these objectives. However, from a larger perspective, the future of the relationship between research and practice is an issue that requires the attention of both academic and professional psychology if we are to achieve our common goals as psychologists.

Will centers for psychological services of the type described by Fox and Rodgers in their chapter and by Albee at the Chicago conference (Hoch et al., 1966) be developed? As settings administered by psychologists for both service delivery and training, these centers would be administratively autonomous in the mental health care delivery system, unlike the settings in which clinical psychologists traditionally have received training and worked professionally. There appears to be potential benefit to the integration of education in professional psychology, as well as to the autonomy of professional psychology, in the establishment of centers for psychological services.

Will the number of programs in professional psychology continue to grow and will existing programs thrive? The answer to this question depends, in large part, on the employability of the increased numbers of professional psychologists generated by these programs. The data reviewed earlier in this chapter suggest that there may be only a limited number of employment opportunities in traditional mental health careers. If a national health insurance legislation is adopted, the policies for reimbursement will have a major effect on the job market. Whether, as Dr. Peterson envisions, professional psychologists will create new career opportunities remains to be seen.

The availability of employment may well have a differential effect on educational programs in the various organizational settings. If independent professional schools, especially profit-making schools, need to have large numbers of students in order to survive, then these programs may be affected the most by the economic contingencies. University-based schools and programs can probably survive with smaller numbers of students and, thus, be less vulnerable to the economic contingencies.

Another factor that may influence the fate of the university-based programs is the relationship between academic and professional psychology. An incompatibility between the values of those two subcultures has been commented on by Fishman and Peterson. Historically, academic psychologists have not had an investment in the education of professional psychologists. This difference in priorities appears to have resulted in the moratorium on admissions in the Psy.D. Program at the University of Illinois. The different values of academic and professional psychology are more likely to result in problems for university-based programs located within academic departments of psychology than for university-based schools of professional psychology.

The most pressing unsolved problem in the quality control of education in professional psychology is the issue of how standards will be enforced. The state laws that govern licensure for the practice of psychology determine, in the final analysis, the standards for the education of professional psychologists. The licensure laws vary considerably from state to state, so there is great inconsistency in the educational standards that are enforced. A solution to this problem is the proposed National Commission on Education and Credentialing in Psychology (Wellner, note 6). A national commission would be able to facilitate the adoption of licensure laws that are consistent from state to state and consistent with the accreditation criteria of the APA.

Conclusion

The resolutions adopted by the conference at Virginia Beach do not provide solutions to the problems confronting professional psychology. They do, however, identify some of the questions that must be answered, and heighten our awareness of the need for evaluative research directed at finding the answers.

As Hoch, Ross, and Winder (1966) have suggested, a conference may be understood as a response to forces both inside and outside the profession. Within psychology, the rapid proliferation of programs in professional psychology had resulted in concern that large numbers of inadequately educated practitioners might be produced, to the detriment of psychological services and at the expense of the public trust of psychology. Outside of the profession there had been, in state and federal legislation, a growing recognition of professional psychology as an autonomous provider of mental health services. The conference at Virginia Beach, then, was a response to the pressing need for the control of the quality of educational programs in professional psychology in order that psychology reach its potential as an independent mental health care provider.

Note

1. This estimate is higher than an estimate (approximately 8,000) based on the data presented in Dr. Caddy's chapter. This discrepancy in the estimates calls attention to a need for more accurate assessments of the number of doctoral students in professional psychology.

Reference Notes

1. Wellner, A. M., & Mills, D. H. *How many health service providers in psychology? Finally an answer* (Register Research Report No. 1). Unpublished

report, Council for the National Register of Health Service Providers in Psychology, 1977.
2. VandenBos, G., Nelson, S., Stapp, J., Olmedo, E., Coates, D., & Batchelor, W. *Memorandum to M. Pallak, APA Executive Officer, re: APA input to NIMH regarding planning for mental health personnel development.* Unpublished report, American Psychological Association, September, 27, 1979.
3. Richards, J. M., Jr. "The distribution of psychology graduate students in the United States." Unpublished manuscript, Center for Social Organization of Schools, Johns Hopkins University, 1979.
4. Meyer, M, University of Florida. Personal communication, February, 22, 1980.
5. Arnold, P., Office of Professional Affairs, American Psychological Association. Personal communication, March 13, 1980.
6. Wellner, A. M. (Ed.) "Education and credentialing in psychology." Unpublished report, Steering Committee for a Proposal for a National Commission on Education and Credentialing in Psychology, American Psychological Association, May 1978.

References

Albee, G. W. *Mental health manpower trends.* New York: Basic Books, 1969.

Albee, G. W. Conceptual models and manpower requirements in psychology. *American Psychologist,* 1968, *23,* 317-20.

Albee, G. W. Preventing prevention. *APA Monitor,* May 1979, p. 2.

American Psychological Association. *Standards for providers of psychological services* (Rev. Ed). Washington, D. C.: Author, 1977.

American Psychological Association. *Criteria for accreditation of doctoral training programs and internships in professional psychology.* Washington, D. C.: Author, 1979.

American Psychological Association Task Force on Continuing Evaluation in National Health Insurance. Continuing evaluation and accountability controls for a national health insurance program. *American Psychologist,* 1978, *33,* 305-13.

Dohrenwend, B. P., & Dohrenwend, B. S. Social and cultural influences on psychopathology. *Annual Review of Psychology,* 1974, *25,* 417-52.

Gottfredson, G. D., & Dyer, S. E. Health service providers in psychology, *American Psychologist,* 1978, *33,* 314-38.

Hoch, E. L., Ross, A. O. & Winder, C. L. *Professional preparation of clinical psychologists.* Washington, D. C.: American Psychological Association, 1966.

Korchin, S. J. *Modern clinical psychology.* New York: Basic Books, 1976.

Korman, M. (Ed.) *Levels and patterns of professional training in psychology.* Washington, D. C.: American Psychological Association, 1976.

Liptzin, B. Supply, demand, and projected need for psychiatrists and other mental health manpower: An analytic paper. In D. M. Kole (Ed.), *Report of the ADAMHA manpower policy analysis task force, Vol. II.* Washington, D. C. Alcohol, Drug Abuse, and Mental Health Administration, 1978.

Mills, D. H., Wellner, A. M., & VandenBos, G. R. The National Register survey: The first comprehensive study of all licensed/certified psychologists. In

C. A. Kiesler, N. A. Cummings, & G. R. VandenBos (Eds.), *Psychology and national health insurance: A sourcebook.* Washington, D. C.: American Psychological Association, 1979.

Nyman, L. Some odds on getting into Ph.D. programs in clinical and counseling psychology. *American Psychologist,* 1973, *28,* 934-35.

Polonsky, I., Fox, R. E., Wiens, A. N. Dixon, T. R., Freedman, M. B., & Shapiro, D. H. Psychology in action: Models, modes, and standards of professional training: An invited interaction. *American Psychologist,* 1979, *34,* 339-49.

Richards, J. M., & Gottfredson, G. D. Geographic distribution of U.S. psychologists: A human ecological analysis. *American Psychologist,* 1978, *33,* 1-9.

United States President's Commission on Mental Health. *Report to the President from the President's Commission on Mental Health.* Washington, D. C.: U. S. Government Printing Office, 1978.

ALSO AVAILABLE

THE RUTGERS PROFESSIONAL PSYCHOLOGY REVIEW
DECEMBER, 1980

CREDENTIALING PROCEDURES IN PROFESSIONAL PSYCHOLOGY

Margaret M. Eaton and Frances P. Snepp, Editors

Table of Contents

Copies may be obtained for $3 each from the Editor, RUTGERS PRO-FESSIONAL PSYCHOLOGY REVIEW, Graduate School of Applied and Professional Psychology, Busch Campus, Rutgers—The State University, New Brunswick, New Jersey 08903